THE AFRICAN
AFRICAN
Baobab

THE
AFRICAN
Baobab

Rupert Watson

Struik Publishers
(a division of New Holland Publishing
  (South Africa) (Pty) Ltd)
Cornelis Struik House
80 McKenzie Street
Cape Town 8001

New Holland Publishing is a division of
  Johnnic Communications Ltd

Visit us at **www.struik.co.za**
Log on to our photographic website
  www.imagesofafrica.co.za for an African experience.

First published in 2007

ISBN 9781770074309

Publishing manager: Pippa Parker
Managing editor: Helen de Villiers
Editor: Colette Alves
Designer: Janice Evans

Cartographer: James Whitelaw
Proofreader: Tessa Kennedy
Indexer: Mary Lennox

Reproduction by Hirt & Carter Cape (Pty) Ltd
Printed and bound by Tien Wah Press (Pte)
  Limited, Singapore

PHOTOGRAPHIC CREDITS
David Baum – pp 12 (top right), 12 (bottom right),
55 (bottom right), 137 (top right); Carol Beckwith/
Angela Fisher – p 166; Mary Ann Burris – author photo;
Alec Campbell – pp 188–9; Peter Davey – pp 55 (top
left), 127 (top right); Nigel Dennis/IOA – pp 29, 106–7;
Malcolm Linton – pp 134, 161, 200; Oscar Mann – pp 157,
165; Ian Michler/IOA – half title page; John Millard –
p 121; Nigel Pavitt – cover, title page, pp 197, 198;
Sally Perry – pp 154–5; Peter and Beverly Pickford – p 28
(bottom); Ariadne van Zandbergen/IOA – pp 6–7;
Philip Walwyn – p 43; Titia Warndorff – p 137 (bottom
left); Nigel Winser – p 15
Foiled image on cloth cover – from Prospero Alpini's *De plantis
Aegypti liber*, with permission from Afriterra Foundation

Contents

CHAPTER ONE
Bu hobab

Baobab trees are living
monuments, the oldest natural
things in Africa, outlasting every
plant and animal around them.
These trees have evolved
formidable resilience in order
to survive in some of the driest,
rockiest areas of this continent. Yet,
for all the hostility of much of their
habitat, African baobabs live longer
and grow larger than most other
trees in the world. That is the great
paradox of their existence.

PREVIOUS PAGES: Occasionally, baobabs grow so close to each other that the branches almost touch, proclaiming the success of their species against seemingly daunting odds.
ABOVE: Baobabs essentially grow alone, often, like this one in Kenya's Tsavo West National Park, far from others.

Solitary trees

Trees as huge as baobabs would seem to belong in forests. There, trees grow branch to branch, nourished by their decaying leaves, collectively protecting each other from the forces of wind and storm, and providing shade, shelter and succour for new saplings. Yet baobabs are solitary trees, shunning the mutual support system of the woodlands. They are also remarkably thirsty trees and, to satisfy that thirst, need space to stretch their roots and suck moisture into their huge water-bloated trunks.

Sometimes baobabs grow close to one another, almost close enough for branches to touch, and certainly for roots to meet and compete in their subterranean quest for liquid. These more closely grouped trees have all survived the early accidents of seed dispersal that brought them together, yet this still does not make them trees of a community. They survive despite, not because of, the nearness of their fellows.

Baobabs dotted the African savanna while our ancestors still lolloped along on four legs. The trees would have provided them with easily gathered fruit, while branches gave shelter from rain, sun and predators. As man gradually started to stand upright (some four million years ago), it freed up his hands to shape tools and may also have freed up his mind to start thinking 'how' and 'why' about his world. Then he may have begun to harvest honey from the bees' nests in the trees, to appreciate the goodness in the leaves, and to use hollow trees as cave-like homes.

Probably not until much later, when *Homo* was *erectus*, even *sapiens*, did he first entertain vague thoughts of greater, unseen forces outside his earthly realm. The world of primitive African man spread as far as his furthest travels. The biggest thing that moved in it was the elephant, and the biggest living thing that didn't was the baobab. The trees were as near to permanent as any living thing could be. If any plant or animal were to inspire notions of animism or religion, and to offer resting places for spirits or gods, surely it would be the baobab.

Creation

While early animistic credos imbued baobabs with spirits of their own, it probably needed belief in a god to prompt theories of their creation.

In most myths of baobab creation the tree is seen to be standing on its head, roots in the air – the ultimate 'upside-down tree'. A popular legend has it that one of the first trees God created was the baobab. When it saw the next tree, a slender palm, it started grumbling that it should be taller. God heeded the baobab's complaint, but no sooner had the tree grown to reach the palm's tops, than it began to covet the flame tree's spectacular flowers. But when it, too, produced flowers, this was still not enough for the baobab. Next, it moaned that, unlike the fig, it had no fruit. This was too much, even for God, and in a rage he wrenched the baobab out of the ground and dashed it back in, head first.

The Giriama on the Kenyan coast have a different story to tell. They say that the sweltering devil lay down to rest in the shade of a baobab tree. Enraged to find it leafless, as the tree is for nearly two thirds of the year, the devil tore it out of the ground and replanted it upside down. Further south, Bushmen dance the story of the baobab's creation by the Great Spirit, who, according to

their folklore, gave a different species of tree to every animal. The last at this great arboreal share-out was the hyaena, who was so dissatisfied at being handed the baobab that it slammed the tree into the ground upside down.

ABOVE: The species is repeatedly described as appearing to grow with its roots in the air.
OVERLEAF: Baobabs are sometimes called 'upside-down trees', and David Livingstone thought they resembled upturned carrots.

It is difficult to recognize young baobab trees because their leaf configuration differs from that of adult trees.

Adansonia perrieri is one of six species of baobab indigenous to Madagascar. Its flowers are pollinated mainly by hawkmoths in the early evening.

The scientific theories regarding the baobab's emergence on Earth are much more prosaic, and almost as speculative. Pachyderms of the plant kingdom – like some of the great thick-skinned mammals still living around them – baobabs also look like forgotten relicts of a former age. It takes no great leap of imagination to visualize dinosaurs rubbing their wrinkled hides along the equally wrinkled bark of the trees, although, in fact, dinosaurs were long gone from this planet by the time baobabs evolved.

With a baobab generation spanning well over 100 years, perhaps much more, the tree's response to environmental shifts is inevitably far more leisurely than that of shorter-lived plants. Yet, while the march of change may have been slow, the genus *Adansonia* has not halted in its evolutionary tracks, like coelacanths, hagfish and cycads have done. In addition to *Adansonia digitata* (the baobab of Africa and of this book), botanists currently recognize seven other well-described species: one in Australia and six in that living laboratory of evolution, Madagascar.

The baobab genus

With so many baobab species, the land that is now Madagascar is most likely the ancestral home of the genus, and the source of its diversification. Today, Malagasy baobabs are largely confined to the island's west coast, and its northern and southern tips. All these species are sufficiently closely related to belong to the genus *Adansonia*, and are distinguished by differences in trunk size, leaf shape and flower colour.

Adansonia rubrostipa is another of Madagascar's spectacular baobabs, also pollinated by hawkmoths.

The lofty *A. grandidieri* and *A. suarezensis* are grouped together into a subgenus, distinguished from the others by, among other things, large seeds, winter flowering, classic flat-topped crowns and thin-shelled pods, which usually break open when they hit the ground.

The other four Malagasy species, *A. perrieri*, *A. madagascariensis*, *A. za*, and *A. rubrostipa*, are characterized, along with micro-differences in the shapes and colours of their exquisite flowers, by blooming in summer and having pods with much thicker shells. Size and shape of trunk vary both between and within species. Some are shorter, squatter trees with more of an African baobab look; others display the classical cylindrical figures of *grandidieri*.

A. grandidieri is the most photographed of all the species in Madagascar. Those near Morandava, on the island's west coast, grace the covers of guidebooks, as well as the memories of visitors who have passed between them along the dirt road to Kirindy Forest Reserve. These same-sized trees, with cylindrical trunks, topped with tufts of horizontal branches, look as if they have been planted out along an avenue leading to a stately Malagasy home. They are, however, relics of thick forest that has been slashed and burnt.

Closer to Kirindy, *rubrostipa* begins to replace *grandidieri* in a scrubby, less modified landscape. A few kilometres down a sandy side track is the celebrated '*baobab amoureuse*' with its two trunks and entwining branches locked in a centuries'

Perhaps the most photographed baobabs in the world, Madagascar's *Adansonia grandidieri* on the road to Kirindy.

long embrace. Back to the main road and on towards the Reserve, scrub gives way to true forest and *A. za* is the dominant species. In early January, it is in full, magnificent bloom, and fallen, yet still fragrant, yellow flowers cover the ground around the tree trunks, fine lines of red streaking both petals and stamens.

Being little known outside their native island, none of the species is identified by any European sobriquet, other than the catch-all, 'baobab'. Local names tend not to distinguish between different species either, and *'renala'* ('mother of the forest') refers to all the baobabs in particular areas, irrespective of species.

The Australian boab

The northwest corner of Australia is home to the most intriguing member of *Adansonia* – at least in terms of how it got where it is. *A. gibbosa* is stumpier than its African relative, although still with a large enough girth for hollow specimens to have been used to incarcerate prisoners. This tree grows around Kimberley and the Victoria River, usually on rocky outcrops, and looks just as prehistoric in its barren Australian landscape as do the baobabs in Africa.

The 'boab', 'gouty-stemmed tree', 'bottle tree' or even 'dead rat tree' (presumably referring to the pendulous fruit) was first brought to the attention of scientists in Europe by Allan Cunningham, on-board naturalist on HMC *Mermaid* during its survey of Australia's west coast between 1818 and 1822. Cunningham initially ascribed the boab to the genus *Capparis* (*C. gibbosa*), perhaps reluctant to believe there could possibly be baobabs in Australia. Once acknowledged as a baobab, it spent some years as *Adansonia gregorii*, briefly illuminating the name of A C Gregory, commander of the 1855 North Australia Exploring Expedition. However, the rules of taxonomic priority, and some good sense, have prevailed, and the tree has reverted to its earlier, more appropriate, species name of *gibbosa*, meaning 'swollen'. As it so often fails to do, taxonomy has at least used half the Latin appellation to describe something about the tree.

Baobab dispersal

With their nearest relatives in Madagascar and mainland Africa, these Australian boabs beg an explanation for their presence in northwestern Australia. It is now commonly accepted that Africa, Madagascar, India, Antarctica and Australasia were all part of the great continuous landmass of Gondwanaland 160 million years ago. The simplest explanation for boabs being where they are today is that when that great slab of earth and rock that was Australia and Antarctica broke off and headed southwards, it carried away baobab ancestors, which eventually evolved into modern boabs. The alternative theory posits that millions of years later, seed pods floated across the ocean to the Australian subcontinent, which by then was more or less where it is now. This entailed pods bobbing thousands of miles over the water, eventually to arrive on a foreign shore receptive enough to enable a few seeds to germinate.

Both ideas strain the imagination, although according to current thinking the latter seems the less unlikely. If baobabs existed before the break-up of Gondwanaland, they should be well spread throughout modern equatorial landmasses, but they are not. One would particularly expect to find them naturally distributed throughout India and the Arabian peninsula. However, while a few trees are scattered across these areas, man, rather than continental drift, seems more likely to have brought them there.

Because their wood contains so much water, and fallen baobabs decompose so quickly, the trees are poor fossilizers. The oldest African fossil

Australian boabs are smaller than their African relatives and have evolved to survive in equally harsh environments.

records of other, harder-wooded baobab relatives date back far enough to suggest the family was not around when Gondwanaland began breaking up. This adds support to the theory that seeds spread from one continent to another much later. So does the unlikelihood of baobabs surviving the lengthy period that Australia and Antarctica spent joined together, far south of the equator – a time during which a lot of the vegetation the landmass had inherited from its ancestral connection to Africa was killed off. Australia was then open for repopulation with new plant life once it began edging further north again on its own.

So, bizarre though it may seem, the balance of evidence favours baobab fruit finding its way over the sea from Madagascar, not only to Australia, but also most likely to Africa. Malagasy baobabs are often found near rivers, suggesting their seeds are well adapted to water dispersal. Perhaps around 30 million years ago some ancestral baobab dropped pods into a river, which carried them out into the open ocean. Most of Madagascar's baobabs grow down the island's west coast, therefore reaching Africa was a fairly uncomplicated journey for seed pods. Australia is far away, even for a well-waterproofed pod propelled by favourable winds and currents, and populating it with baobabs could have been at least a two-staged process. Pods may have first made landfall on islands en route, which are now submerged by higher water levels, with seeds from these new colonies finally making it to Australia.

The bombax (*Chorisia speciosa*) is one of the baobab's closest relatives and grows easily outside its native Brazil. Unlike the baobab, bombax pods burst open on the tree, and wind disperses the seeds.

Once there, a few more crucial metres remained to be covered, requiring as fortuitous a combination of events as the trans-oceanic odyssey. The contents of the pods had to get over the bare sand of the high-water mark into more receptive soils beyond. Earthquakes or volcanic eruptions cause exceptional waves. Tsunamis or other rogue waves – unique combinations of tides and winds – come rolling in to almost any coastline, providing that critical nudge inland that finally allows a seed to germinate on foreign soil. And if huge waves didn't send seeds far inland, perhaps ancestral marsupials foraged along the beach picking up exotic-looking seed packages and scampering off into the undergrowth to examine them in peace.

The genus *Adansonia*'s nearest relatives are the other members of the Bombacaceae family. Small by plant family standards, Bombacaceae's boundaries are ill-defined and some taxonomists have clumped it back into Malvaceae (whose best-known genus is *Hibiscus*), from which it was originally split in 1822. The closest of all trees to the baobabs, and sometimes grouped into the same subfamily, is the genus *Chorisia*, whose flag bearer is the spectacular, pink-flowered, spiny-trunked bombax (*C. speciosa*). It may be no surprise that the lightweight balsa tree (*Ochroma pyramidale*) is a member of Bombacaceae, as is the kapok (*Ceiba pentandra*), which, like the African baobab, is pollinated by bats.

Discovering the baobab

The history of geographical exploration and the parallel progress of the science of taxonomy brim with 'discoveries'. For the most part, 'discovery' is a euphemism for revealing to the western world places, plants and animals with which other humans have long been familiar. Yet only by collating the mass of these revelations was it possible to fit them into a grander design. Only when travellers ventured beyond their immediate horizons could plants and animals take their place in wider geographical or scientific contexts.

The first written reference to the tree that was to become known as a baobab does not come from the pen of any European explorer, but from that of the scribe of the indefatigable traveller, Ibn Battuta, born in Tangiers around 1304. After making his hajj to Mecca he took to using the city as a base for journeys into India, down the coast of East Africa, as well as to Turkey and through the Middle East. It would be nearly 25 years before

The kapok tree is native to Central and South America. Like the baobab, it has digitate (five-fingered) leaves, and its widely spaced branches make it easy for pollinating bats to reach the flowers.

he returned to Tangiers and, having done so, he was soon back on his camel, heading south, through the Sahara to Timbuktu and into the Niger basin.

More of a social than natural historian, Ibn Battuta's account of the interaction between Islam and animism is particularly fascinating. Still, naturalist or not, on his way to the Kingdom of Mali in 1353, he found:

'The road has many trees of great age and size; a caravan can shelter under a single one of them. Some of them have no branches or leaves but the trunk gives enough shade to shelter men. Some of these trees have rotted inside and rainwater has collected there, as if it were a well. People drink this water. In some of these trees are bees and honey, which people collect.'

Ibn Battuta had been dead almost a hundred years before Europeans, particularly the Portuguese with their long-established maritime traditions, began opening up the coast of Africa. Driven by the competitive urge to dominate Venetian traders, these early sailors launched their expeditions with aspirations of commercial empire building rather than of exploring the natural world. Nonetheless, baobabs, growing so huge and close to the sea, proved impossible to ignore.

In 1448, Gomes Eannes de Azurara, exploring the islands of Guinea-Bissau, came across a tree he subsequently described in *Plantas Uteis de Africa Portugesa* as being 108 hands in circumference. It needs no name for us to guess its identity, nor does the tree described six years later by Alvise Ca' da Mosto (generally remembered as 'Cadamosto') during his second voyage down the West African coast. Having passed Cape Verde, he turned into the Gambia River, and a few miles upstream found the banks:

'. . . covered with numerous and very large trees which are everywhere throughout the country. Concerning the size of these, I may say that, at a spring near the river bank from which we drew water, there was a very great and broad tree; its height, however, was not in proportion to its size, for while we judged it to be about twenty paces high we found the girth by measurement to be about seventeen paces round the foot. It was hollow in many places, and its branches were very large so that they threw a deep shade around.'

More observant travellers looked beyond the shapes and sizes of plants and animals to the ways in which the local people made use of them. As the Renaissance drew to a close, botanical research was largely motivated by the search for better drugs with which to treat wealthy Europeans. Prospero Alpini was an Italian herbalist and physician from Venice who spent three years in Cairo at the end of the sixteenth century, ostensibly acting as the private doctor to the Italian consul. The consul's health obviously held up well, because this sinecure seems to have given Alpini much spare time. This he devoted to botanical study, particularly of the sexual life of the date palm. His collected observations culminated in the publication of *De*

MICHEL ADANSON
(Botaniste)
Membre de l'Académie des Sciences,
Né à Aix (B. du Rhône) le 7 Avril 1727,
Mort à Paris le 3 Aoust 1806.

Michel Adanson, the French botanist after whom the genus takes its name.
(With permission, Hunt Institute for Botanical Documentation)

plantis Aegypti liber (1592), which contained the first detailed written description of the baobab. Alpini had seen the fruit selling in the Cairo souks under the Arabic name *bu hobab*, which, roughly translated, means 'having many seeds'.

Baobab classification

As the tempo of overseas exploration increased, specimens of fauna and flora poured into infant centres of research for analyzing and comparing, recording and naming, finding sameness and difference. To give this plethora of new information a semblance of order, a system of grouping and naming was vital. And so taxonomy was born – first as an art, then a science, now a biological necessity. The tradition of classification goes back to Aristotle, but not until John Ray catalogued over 18 000 plant species in *The Wisdom of God Manifested in the Works of Creation* (1691) were species first arranged in some sort of hierarchical order. As a clergyman, his rigid belief in the biblical theory of Creation is not surprising, although later in life both he and his scientific successor, Carl Linnaeus, began to doubt the wisdom of denying any possibility of the emergence of new species. Ray defined the concept of a species and Linnaeus then developed the idea of classifying each one, using a binomial system of nomenclature focused on similarities between them.

Linnaeus did a lot of first-hand research in his native Sweden. For specimens and descriptions from elsewhere in the world he relied upon submissions from observant travellers. One of these was Michel Adanson – a French naturalist, small in stature, with vast energy, a huge head and masses of red hair. By dint of contacts and enthusiasm, Adanson had found himself a four-year posting with the *Compagnie de L'Occident et des Indes*, arriving in 1749 to research the natural resources of what is now Senegal.

Adanson's surprise on first seeing a baobab shows how unprepared he was for this botanical bombshell. In his *Histoire naturelle du Senegal* (1757), published in Paris and translated by 'an English Gentleman' two years later, he relates:

> *They carried me to a particular spot where I saw a herd of antelopes; but I laid a-side all thoughts of sport, as soon as I perceived a tree of a prodigious thickness, which drew my whole attention. This was a calabash-tree, which the Jaloffes call goui in their language. There was nothing extraordinary in its height; for it was only about sixty feet: but its trunk was of a prodigious thickness.'*

After measuring the branches, roots and trunks of other trees he concluded that 'in short the whole of this calabash tree seemed to form a forest in itself'. And with these descriptions began the baobab's remarkably brief and, by the standards of the time, uncontroversial, introduction to modern science. Before returning from his African travels in 1754, Adanson was able to send an account of the baobab to his mentor in France, Bernard Jussieu, who had created the Trianon Gardens for Louis XV. This account in turn found its way to Linnaeus in Sweden in time for inclusion in *Species Plantarum*, published while Adanson was still in Africa.

Linnaeus had first propounded his binomial system of classification in *Systema Naturae* in 1735,

The classic five-fingered leaf that provides the African baobab with its species name, *digitata*.

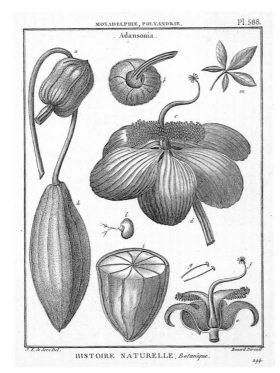

One of the first scientific illustrations of the baobab, this appeared in the volume of engravings accompanying the *Dictionnaire de botanique*, by J B P A Lamarck, published in Paris in 1796. Lamarck was the first person to produce a reasoned theory of evolution.
(With permission, Hunt Institute for Botanical Documentation)

the fruit described by Alpini in the Cairo souk, he continued to advance 'baobab' as a more appropriate generic tag. Linnaeus was not to be deterred, and ultimately carved Adanson's name in the stone tablets of taxonomy by repeating the name *Adansonia digitata* in the 10th and definitive edition of *Systema Naturae* (1759).

Ironically, Adanson remained opposed to the Linnaean system of taxonomy. He spent much of his later working life trying to gather support for a massive 27-volume publication entitled *Universal Order of Nature*, which would have set him on a classification collision course with Linnaeus. Such encouragement as he received from his colleagues quickly evaporated in the heat of the Revolution, during which Adanson lost almost everything but his head, his formidable mental energies finally deserting him in 1806. With the dying words 'Adieu, immortality is not of this world', he requested that one flower from each of the 58 botanical families he had categorized according to his own formula be placed on his coffin.

But immortality *has* shown itself to be of this world, at least in so far as his name lives on in the books of African, Australian and Malagasy trees. *Adansonia digitata* remains the African baobab's Latin name, finding its place in the list of around 350 000 species of plants on Earth, and has had to withstand very little serious attempt to change it. *Adansonia bahobab* and *Baobabus digitata* were both half-heartedly floated as more acceptable alternatives, but too late to overturn the name Linnaeus ascribed to the tree nearly 250 years ago.

There are as many local African words for 'baobab' as there are languages spoken where the trees grow – and a lot more besides, because some tribes distinguish different types of baobab, each of which is given its own distinctive name. The authors of the great compendium of ethnobotanical knowledge, *The Medicinal and*

and there can be no greater testimony to its logical efficacy than that it still endures today. With the first of Madagascar's endemic baobabs only to be scientifically described over 150 years later, the African tree clearly needed its own genus. So, in the Frenchman's absence, and encouraged by Jussieu, Linnaeus chose to Latinize 'Adanson' for the generic name, rather than Alpini or any of the many others who had earlier described the tree.

On his return to France, Adanson was overawed by the honour of finding his name incorporated into the formal description of the baobab. Having connected the tree with

Poisonous Plants of Southern and Eastern Africa, include 68 vernacular names, and there are probably just as many others missing from the list. Particularly striking is the fact that at least a quarter of the words on the list are variations on the *mbuyu* or *muyu* theme, showing the linguistic links between the present-day fragments of the great Bantu diaspora. In Swahili, the lingua franca of East Africa, baobab is *mbuyu*, and this echoes down Tanzania in the tongues of Bondei, Digo, Nyakusa, Zigula and Shambala, through Zimbabwe in Lozi, Karanga, Zezuru and Shona. Like a trans-continental game of Chinese whispers, the word finally emerges at the southern end of the baobab's range in the Limpopo province, in Venda language, as *muvhuyu*.

The names 'monkey-bread tree' and, in Francophone Africa, *'pain de singe'* reflect the fondness of baboons, and any other monkeys strong enough to open the seed pods, for the pith inside.

Thomas Baines painted this fine watercolour of a baobab in full leaf near Lake Ngami in northern Botswana in December 1861.

(With permission, Royal Botanic Gardens, Kew)

The essence of the baobab is in its shape, which is particularly distinctive when silhouetted by the setting sun.

Colloquial names have the licence to describe the very essence of a plant or animal with a lyricism not open to simple nouns, although 'baobab' does at least focus on the tree's many-seeded fruit. Most other names single out the white floury pith surrounding the seeds, which monkeys are not alone in enjoying. Several European names derive from the popularity of the pith, as either a refreshing drink – 'lemonade tree' – or a substitute for tartaric acid – 'cream-of-tartar tree' (*kremetartboom* in Afrikaans) or 'Ethiopian sour gourd'. However, none of these epithets has quite the poetry of the French *arbre de mille ans* (tree of a thousand years).

It would be at least a hundred years after Adanson's description formalized the baobab's scientific existence before British explorers began penetrating into eastern and southern Africa. They were unlikely to have been aware of the tree's existence as they embarked, unless they had read about it. First gracing bookshop windows in 1857, David Livingstone's *Missionary Travels* was one of the earliest accounts of African exploration and contained a two-page passage on the tree, which was clearly the same tree Adanson had found in West Africa.

Whether most travellers recognized baobabs as such, or only identified them on their return home, their ingenuous astonishment on first seeing the trees reverberates throughout one description after another. Typical was James Chapman in *Travels in the Interior of South Africa*. In

1852, accompanied by Thomas Baines, he found himself in northern Botswana, confronting one of his first baobabs:

*'We were lost in amazement, truly,
at the stupendous grandeur of this
mighty monarch of the forest, in
comparison with which the largest
of hundreds of surrounding palm
trees sunk into apparent insignificance.'*

This tree is indeed a massive specimen, now protected under Botswana's Monuments and Relics Act. Its silhouette towers over the nearby fan palms (*Hyphaene petersiana*) and it still lures exhausted or inquisitive travellers to its shade.

The bewildering variety in the shapes and sizes of both the trunks and fruit of baobabs gave several hopefuls enough reason to think they had found something fundamentally different from the tree described by Michel Adanson. The huge distance between the tropical coasts of East and West Africa, on both of which baobabs flourish, lent definite weight to the possibility of there being more than one species. Physical distance is often a precursor to genetic distance and, if populations have been separated long enough, their distinctive evolutionary trails will eventually begin to distinguish them.

In 1860 Britain's armchair explorers were reading *The Lake Regions of Central Africa* by Richard Burton. This polymath knew exactly what a baobab was when he wrote about it, and his extraordinary breadth of experience enabled him to make connections and comparisons nobody else possibly could. His name needed no immortalizing in a subspecies of *Adansonia digitata*, which makes his observations on the possibility of subspecific differences all the more valid:

*'There appear to be two variations
of this tree, similar in bole but differing
in foliage and in general appearance.
The normal Mbuyu has a long leaf,
and the drooping outline of the mass
is convex; the rarer, observed only upon
the Usagara Mountains, has a small
leaf, in colour like the wild indigo,
and the arms striking upwards
assume the appearance of a bowl.'*

However, the rush to divide up the species would be short-lived. A year before the publication of Burton's book, Charles Darwin had thrown the rock of *The Origin of Species by Means of Natural Selection* into the pool of scientific philosophy. Species classification would never be the same again, as taxonomy was forced to look back over its shoulder to common ancestry, rather than at physical distinctions. So began a hundred years of clumping hitherto separated races, subspecies, even species, together again. Now, with DNA analysis fast becoming cheaper and quicker, the wheel could be turning full circle, as microbiology vindicates the species splitters after all.

While scientists are counting chromosomes and comparing DNA, the Dogon and Bambara people in Mali are recognizing differences in bark colour, sufficient to give black-, grey- and red-barked baobabs different names. The distinctions in Mali extend beyond bark colour, as they do elsewhere in Africa, to fruit taste and suitability of bark fibre for ropes and baskets. In Botswana, a connection is made between pink-skinned trees and sweet pith, as it is in Tanzania by some of the Hadzabe.

As is often the case, science seems to be chasing after tradition.

The differences in shapes and sizes of trunks prompted many early European explorers to think they had found new subspecies, or even species, of baobab.

CHAPTER TWO

A tree of Africa

Baobabs are quintessentially African trees. It is possible they do not occur naturally anywhere beyond the continental mainland and some of its outlying islands. However, the outline of the species map is indistinct, and we will never know for sure whether some of the flourishing colonies along its edges are due to the mobility of mankind, or to the randomness of natural seed dispersal.

Native range of the trees

Roughly, indigenous baobabs grow naturally throughout continental Africa between the latitudes of 16° N and 26° S. The waterless wastes of the Sahara push down on the northern edges of their range and, although Khartoum is almost within the baobab's native area, and seed pods are easily bought in the market, the trees found there are cultivated. To the south, the baobab's approximate limits are marked by the Limpopo basin in the east, and a line through northern Namibia in the west.

By overlaying the tree's optimum rainfall, temperature and altitude on this great belt of tropical Africa, as well as preferred drainage, soil types and other environmental influences, a very disjointed distribution map emerges. The most distinctive feature is the huge unmarked space in the centre of the continent where no baobabs grow, and which effectively splits northern baobabs into two separate populations.

Being so widespread, baobabs are components of many different ecosystems, testifying to their tolerance of varying temperature, rainfall and soil type. The baobab's habitats are so diverse that it is almost easier to define the trees' requirements by where they cannot live, than where they can.

PREVIOUS PAGES: Baobabs in Kenya's Tsavo National Park were devastated by elephants in the second half of the twentieth century, and in many areas the only ones left are growing on hillsides.
ABOVE: The essence of Africa.
BELOW: The Himba live in Kaokoland in northwestern Namibia, where temperature can vary from cold to very hot. Baobabs are common over much of the country, although the next generation of trees is threatened by the overgrazing of domestic animals.

There is no upper limit to the temperatures baobabs can survive, provided their soil and rainfall requirements are met. They grow easily in Mauritania and in the lowlands of Eritrea, where human inhabitants swelter in average summer temperatures of well over 30° C. At the other end of the thermometer, the baobab cannot endure the recurring spells of sustained frost that effectively demarcate much of its southern limits. This is not to say that baobabs, particularly mature specimens, cannot live through occasional freezing spells. Some of the biggest baobabs in Africa grow near Tsumkwe in northeastern Namibia, where temperatures regularly fall well below zero several nights in a row.

It takes more than just lack of frost to create a suitable environment for baobabs. They cover the northern slopes of the Soutpansberg mountains of South Africa, spreading all the way down through mopane woodland to the Limpopo River. There being almost none on the southern slopes may be a consequence of differences in sunlight, temperature, rainfall, geology or some other more obscure needs of the tree that are unfulfilled on the shadier side of the mountains. Elsewhere on the continent, particularly in Kenya and Tanzania, the trees are absent from vast tracts of land where, superficially at least, conditions seem ideal.

Nowhere do baobabs grow naturally much above 1 500 m. Yet the trees grow at this height as far north as northern Ethiopia. Around the equator, temperature ranges at higher altitudes are similar to those closer to sea level near the tropics. Why there is no sign of baobabs ever having colonized apparently suitable areas up to 2 000 m on the equator, where it is never anywhere near freezing, remains a mystery. Perhaps many

ABOVE: This baobab is growing in Pafuri, Kruger National Park, which is about as far south as the trees are found.

A baobab in the semi-desert of Eritrea growing at the extreme north of the species range; branches have been cut so leaves can be fed to livestock, while the tree itself is being used as a store for animal fodder.

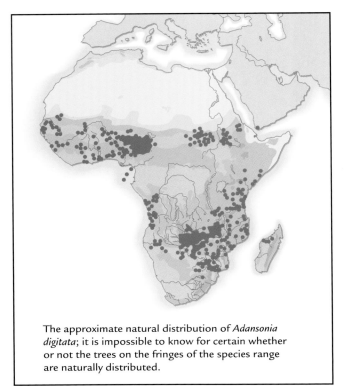

The approximate natural distribution of *Adansonia digitata*; it is impossible to know for certain whether or not the trees on the fringes of the species range are naturally distributed.

On the coast of Kenya, rainfall at Kilifi Plantations' cattle and sisal farm has averaged 1 170 mm over the last 30 years. More than half the year's rain falls in the second quarter, the rest fairly evenly over the next six months. Even when it isn't raining, humidity is high. A hundred kilometres inland, conditions are much harsher for baobabs growing in Tsavo National Park. Drier parts of the park receive 255 mm of rain in most years, often in two distinct seasons, and humidity is minimal. On parts of the west coast of the continent, the struggling baobabs in Mauritania have to survive not only maximum temperatures and extreme water loss, but an average annual rainfall of less than 100 mm, in one short spell.

Too much rain may damn baobabs' chances just as effectively as too little. The maximum they can endure, year after year, seems to be about 1 400 mm (although the specimen in Calcutta's Botanical Garden tolerates a lot more). Baobabs are not forest trees, and young saplings are unable to compete with the luxuriant vegetation that grows in areas of heavy rainfall. This largely explains the great blank in the heart of the African map where the only baobabs occur around human habitations and, as such, are certainly imported.

Soil provides trees with nourishment and support, and its composition is fundamental to successful growth. There are few combinations of rock and soil that baobabs cannot eventually colonize, given suitable temperatures and rainfall. However, soft deep sand is not ideal, as it does not give the tree's roots sufficient support. A tree that appears to be growing successfully on the dunes

months of cool nights are fatal to their fortunes, or long spells of grey damp days too much for tender young seedlings. Maybe there are fewer pollinators or seed dispersers at higher altitudes. If planted in well-drained soil, baobabs will just survive in Nairobi at nearly 2 000 m, and of the two specimens in the Nairobi Arboretum, one looks particularly healthy with four strong trunks, each nearly 10 m tall. Both planted in 1922, neither of the trees has ever flowered.

Temperature is merely one component of the environmental equation. Equally crucial is rainfall, and here the species shows true adaptability. Not only does the baobab survive in areas with very different rainfall averages, it also tolerates the successive years of extreme droughts and raging floods imposed by the vagaries of African weather.

is usually anchored to a layer of denser soil below the sand. With sands and coastlines shifting over time, it may actually have been much further from the sea when first sprouting from its seed.

ABOVE: High tides now wash seaweed over this baobab's roots, although wave erosion is likely to have exposed them over the centuries. Growing so close to the sea, the tree could well be the result of baobab seeds being dispersed by water.
OVERLEAF: Baobabs growing in the middle of Epupa Falls on the Kunene River, which forms the Angola–Namibia border.

Surface soil can sometimes seem almost superfluous. Baobabs often direct their roots down cracks in stony outcrops, gaining good support but very little nutrition. On the tiny islets between the cataracts of the Kunene River's spectacular Epupa Falls in northern Namibia, baobabs appear to live off water alone, their roots probing fissures in the rock in which there is little, if any, soil. Likewise, many trees along the East African coast are growing on no more than a few millimetres of decomposed vegetation, sprinkled over the rocky relics of much higher sea levels, their roots even washed by high water tides.

Given the tree's adaptability to such varied environments, it is impossible to extrapolate ideal natural conditions for baobab growth. Baobabs proclaim their success as a species in different ways. The localized monsters in Tsumkwe or northern Botswana show that a thin layer of sand overlaying a non-porous base of calcrete is an ideal foundation for trees to reach enormous size. Yet the massed ranks of smaller baobabs in the valley of the Great Ruaha River are growing on steep, rocky slopes. And if a species' success was to be judged by a combination of numbers and size, parts of Senegal or the East African coastline seem to offer habitat which is little short of perfect.

Approaching natural baobab country, one is continually struck by the presence of outlying trees, far from the main aggregations – outriders fringing the edges of baobab populations, as if abandoned in the trees' retreat. These may be relics of a much wider distribution, survivors from a different age, hanging on in the face of environmental degradation or warming climate, their ancestors long decayed. Two of Botswana's most famous baobab specimens, Green's and Chapman's, grow 5 km from each other, but otherwise, there seem to be no others within at least a day's walk of those trees.

It would be heartening to feel that some of these isolated trees actually evidence expansions of the baobab's natural range – early colonizers settling new territory rather than relicts staying on as their empire declines. Sadly this doesn't seem to be so. A few seeds spat out by wandering Bushmen or crowds at a rural Zimbabwe bus stop may lead to trees growing where they never grew before. But ultimately, the influence of exploding populations of humans and their livestock on the baobab's fortunes cannot be other than destructive.

This enormous baobab is growing far from any others, right on the edge of baobab territory. Its final collapse will result in a significant contraction in the species' range in Namibia.

The hand of man

Historically, mankind's impact on baobabs has been more positive, and dense clumps where baobabs are otherwise sparsely spread often signify old human habitations. This connection between trees and humans is undeniable, although less clear is whether baobabs attracted people with shade and nourishment, or if the trees are there as a consequence of human activity.

As little as 5 000 years ago giraffes were nibbling acacia branches throughout most of what is now desert. Almost certainly baobabs then grew far up into today's Sahara, before a warming world slowly forced them into retreat. As the limits for both human and baobab survival were pushed southwards, man may have depended on finding areas to live that were already populated with the trees.

Human activity is also likely to have encouraged more trees to grow. Once nomads adopted more settled lifestyles, they would have brought home pods from wild baobabs for food or medicine. Seeds are often sucked for the surrounding pith or the two separated by vigorous stirring. Discarded seeds might have germinated around the villages, helped on their way with slops of dirty washing water.

Europeans frequently remarked upon the connection between baobabs and human habitations. The German Heinrich Barth is one of the unsung heroes of African exploration. He was introduced to Africa in 1849 as a member of a British anti-slavery expedition. His formal mission over, he began travelling on his own, offering most of the Africans along his astounding 19 000 km route around Central Africa and the Sahel their first glimpse of a white face. His five-volume *Travels and Discoveries in North and Central Africa*

Did this baobab emerge from a seed dispersed by human travellers? The road has certainly been there longer than this young tree has.

makes particularly rich reading, and is all the more remarkable for its publication in 1857, when Stanley was only 16 and Burton and Speke had yet to reach Lake Tanganyika. Barth's scientific leanings and powers of observation are evident in his comments:

'Here and there a large leafless Adansonia stretches forth its gigantic arms as if bewailing the desolation spread around, where human beings had formerly subsisted: for the Kuka or baobab likes the dwelling of the negro, and he, on the other hand, can scarcely live without it; for how could he season his simple food without the baobab's young fresh leaves, or sweeten and flavour his drink without the slightly acid pulp wherein the kernels are imbedded?
It has been remarked by travellers that this tree is only found near some dwelling place of man; but I doubt whether we are authorised to regard all those specimens of it which are scattered over the wilds of central Africa as marking the site of former towns.'

ABOVE: Most of the baobabs in Jumba la Mtwana on the Kenya coast are unlikely to have been around in 1450, the estimated date of the town's abandonment.
OVERLEAF: This baobab is growing right on the edge of the salt pans from which most of Kenya's salt is extracted – conditions that hardly seem ideal, yet the tree appears to be perfectly healthy.

In 1924, the writings of F W H Migeod appeared under the title *Through Nigeria to Lake Chad*. The author was an acute observer, focusing as much on the people he encountered along his way as on the plants and animals. He was also a believer in the association between baobabs and human settlements, and remarks on the baobab population in the area around the Benue River in the west, and that the tree . . .

> *'. . . has been imported by the Fulbe into these places and is not indigenous there. The mode of its dissemination is for the fruit to be carried on from the last tree to be eaten, for it is a favourite article of food, and the seeds thrown out germinate. Hence it is practically only in towns that it is found, and if found in the bush usually indicates the former presence of a village or camp.'*

He then suggests, in describing his visit to Yola, in eastern Nigeria, that knowing when humans first settled in a particular area could help age the surrounding baobabs '. . . as it is improbable that any [baobabs] were there before the Fulbe founded the town a hundred years ago when they moved here from Gurin, the parent town'.

This is an interesting contrast to the ideas of the Giriama on the East African coast, who believe that only when a settlement is abandoned will baobabs begin to grow. They suggest that as long as domestic animals are nibbling at anything tender and green, or human and animal feet are flattening the surrounding ground, seedlings will never survive to grow into trees. C W Hobley, writing 'On Baobabs and Ruins' in the 1922 *Journal of the East Africa and Uganda Natural History Society*, reached the same conclusion, that only once 'the place was deserted owing to war or other causes, the bush would cover the area and the more recent baobab seeds would germinate along with other plants'.

Arabs founded their first African trading posts over 1 000 years ago. Many of their early settlements were on islands such as Manda, Zanzibar and Kilwa. Others occupied mainland sites, often several kilometres from the sea. Some of these settlements were abandoned at least 500 years ago, others more recently. It is seldom clear whether the inhabitants were driven away by disease, warfare or water shortages. Mostly, only outlines of foundations remain – heat, rain and rampant vegetation having combined to reduce an ancient township to a few piles of overgrown stones. If it had not been for the towering presence of baobab trees betraying their existence, many of these sites might still lie undiscovered under tangles of creeping greenery.

Clumps of East African coastal baobabs may shade the burial sites of wandering Arab traders and imams. On the very edge of Mikindani Bay, near Tanzania's border with Mozambique, an Islamic holy man is buried in a one-man cemetery under a baobab. The oldest person I could find in the village remembered him praying daily beneath the tree. It seemed a fitting resting place for the man's mortal remains. Here, tree clearly preceded grave, and perhaps also at the spectacular Tongoni Ruins burial ground much further north. There, on the slopes below a tumbledown mosque, are the graves of at least 40 Islamic holy men. On the seaward side of the burial site are three beautiful baobabs, and the gravestones face down between their trunks to the sweep of mangrove-fringed coastline.

It is likely that old slave routes can be charted from strangely sited baobabs – just as borassus (*Borassus aethiopum*), doum (*Hyphaene compressa*)

and other palms are supposed to reveal the ancient migration routes of elephants. Arab slave traders travelling from the coast are sure to have carried baobab fruit with them, just as they did in their boats, spitting out pips along the way and so extending the baobab's range further inland, as well as marking their trails for posterity.

On the bigger island groups further off the coasts of Africa, the origins of healthy populations of baobabs are even less certain. Seed pods are said to have drifted on Indian Ocean currents to Aldabra, nearly 1 000 km from the mainland, and could have reached the Comoros, Mauritius and Réunion in the same way. On the other side of Africa, the Cape Verde Islands are so covered with baobabs it seems they must occur there naturally.

In addition to six endemic baobabs, clumps of *Adansonia digitata* are also found in Madagascar. These trees are nearly all found along the island's west coast, and are so clearly associated with human habitation that little doubt exists as to their introduction by mankind – returning a more evolved form of baobab to its ancestral homeland, and the most likely centre of the genus's original speciation.

Of equally debatable origins are the few trees in Yemen and Oman. The presence of other African tree species in southwestern Arabia suggests baobabs could also have arrived there naturally, rather than in the dhows of Arab sailors.

In India, too, there are enough African baobabs to have caused much speculation on their origins. One of the most telling arguments in favour of a comparatively recent arrival is the lack of a Sanskrit name for the tree, or indeed any name that is not merely a hybrid of two older words with other meanings. *Khurasani imli* is one of the Hindi names for baobab in Uttar Pradesh, which, loosely translated, means the 'foreign tamarind'. Other names incorporate *salmali*, the Sanskrit name for the kapok-like, red silk-cotton tree (*Bombax*

malabaricum). There is no mention of the baobab in ancient Indian floral texts, nor are there long-established uses for any part of the tree. If it really was part of India's botanical heritage, such lack of written record or traditional usage is inconceivable.

If nature did not spread baobabs to India, there must be an explanation for their presence. It is easy to imagine seed pods bobbing over to Yemen, and even Oman is only a short float away compared to Australia, which baobabs probably reached from Madagascar. But if baobabs had got to India by water, they would have established themselves there much earlier. They would also be most common down the west coast of the subcontinent, which they are not. It is more likely that they were imported by Arabs, which is the view of B H Baden-Powell, writing in the *Indian Forester* of 1878/9 that:

> 'The Tree was introduced into India from Tropical Africa (where it is indigenous) by Arab traders. Individual specimens have found their way as far north as Ajmir and the North-West Provinces. In Ajmir it is also called the "Kalp-briksh" or "Wishing Tree".'

This was no more than the generally accepted wisdom of the time, and it is still possible to correlate areas where baobabs are commonest with those parts of India most under the influence of Islam. For thousands of years Arabs traded their way around the Indian Ocean rim, and almost certainly carried baobab fruit with them, probably as an on-board source of vitamin C. In addition to discarding any surplus when they docked, they may also have sought to spread their sources of supply by encouraging Indians to plant the trees for shade, medicine, decoration or food.

The slave trade was the catalyst for the spread of baobabs all over the Caribbean, seed pods coming over on boats during the forced African diaspora. Following their long-held traditions, Arab traders will have carried them as vitamin-rich food for the journey, and also as a prophylactic for scurvy.

What is claimed to be the oldest baobab in Barbados stands near Warrens, once a great plantation house, but now engulfed by the expansion of Bridgetown. *Flora Barbadia* quotes an early European History of the Island suggesting the tree dates from around 1735 and sprouted from a seed brought over from Guinea. The trees are mentioned in an early version of *Flora of Dutch West Indian Islands* as occurring in St Eustatius and St Martin, and they are also found in Trinidad. Guinea seems to have been the source of trees in Tobago too, judging from the baobab's colloquial name there of Guinea Tamarind.

The further away from Africa baobabs grow, the more assured is their exotic status. They thrive in Guyana, on the north coast of South America, and many are now found in southern Florida, the seeds apparently imported from Cuba, and that island's from Haiti. In turn, Haitian baobabs derive from seeds brought over from Africa on slave boats or by immigrants of French descent.

Baobabs need more than just a helping human hand to disperse them if they are to survive very far beyond the tropics. The baobab in the

This baobab grows in the middle of the central square in Basseterre, St Kitts, West Indies; it owes its presence, so far from Africa, to the slave trade.

The trunk of the baobab in St Kitts; the tree is enough of a botanical oddity to merit a name tag to inform the curious.

Kirstenbosch Botanical Gardens outside Cape Town owes its size to the warmth of a glasshouse. The species' exotic status in England has never been in question; its introduction there goes back nearly 300 years, to 1724, when George I was on the throne.

Philip Miller (1691–1771) tended the Botanick Garden in Chelsea for the Worshipful Company of Apothecaries. His *Gardener's Dictionary* went into eight editions, and in the seventh edition (1764) he describes the first importation of baobabs into England:

> *The plants have been many years in England, yet none of them have produced Flowers, so that we are at a loss for the Characters. We have some plants of this sort in several gardens which were raised from Seeds obtained from Grand Cairo in the Year 1724, by the late Dr William Sherrard, many of which were grown to the Height of eighteen Feet; but in the severe Winter of 1740, they were all lost, and since that Time there has not been any of the Seeds brought to England, till the return of Mr Adanson to Paris, who sent some of the Seeds over here, which have succeeded and many of the Plants are now upwards of six Feet high.'*

In tropical botanical gardens all around the world, baobabs display bloated trunks and wrinkled skins to unbelieving visitors. Sometimes, local fruit bats will visit the flowers and ensure that seed pods eventually bedeck the branches of these exotic imports. While such representatives of their species can hardly be said to be extending its range, they certainly create greater public awareness of the existence of this botanical marvel.

Even in Africa the demarcation of baobab territory owes much to human rather than natural history. Further away, particularly in India and the West Indies, the tree flourishes thanks to the early popularity of its fruit, and by most standards is a net gain to its new environment. Whether baobabs are indigenous or exotic, the relationship between man and tree seems, at least for most of their joint existence, to have worked for the benefit of both.

'... baobabs so formidable, gigantic, lofty, monumental, we might as well have been driving among the skyscrapers of Manhattan. Like elephants among other animals, so are baobabs among trees: they have no equals.'
(Ryszard Kapuscinski – *The Shadow of the Sun*)

CHAPTER THREE
Flower and seed

Like animals, plants begin life at the critical moment of conception. Whether baobab, butterfly or baboon, new life only starts when a male cell joins a female, when sperm makes contact with an egg. For butterflies or baboons, copulation is the prelude to conception. For flowering plants, it is pollination – when that great extravagance, the flower, tempts birds, insects and other animals with colour and scent into unconsciously shifting dust from the stamen of one bloom to the stigma of another.

PREVIOUS PAGES: It is difficult to imagine how all the parts of a fully developed flower ever fitted inside the bud.
ABOVE AND OVERLEAF: Ages can differ significantly between members of a single population of baobabs.

Flowers

Young trees need all their energy for growing, and have none to spare for reproduction. Baobabs may be near 30 before they begin diverting vitality into the production of flowers, and their first waxy white blooms appear. These blooms are striking, in both size and design, their magnificence in shining contrast to the stark grey tree that produces them, particularly when flowers appear on bare branches. Programmed by the tree's hormones to stay open for no longer than a single night and into the next morning, these are surely one of nature's more elaborate excesses.

Before a flower breaks open, the petals (corolla) and the other parts deeper inside are squeezed tightly into a spherical bud about the size of a golf ball. The outside of the bud (calyx) is made up of protective, dark greeny-yellow

Pollination is the process of transferring male pollen from stamens to stigma. At the other end of the stigma is the ovary, inside which the egg cells rest. Once deposited on the stigma, pollen shoots down a long tube through the style, the sperm then travelling quickly down the tube to fertilize the eggs. Successful conception quickly becomes evident in the appearance of a tiny pod encasing a capsule of small white seeds.

Baobabs are bisexual, or perfect, in botanical terms, in that there are male stamens and a female style on each flower, unlike unisexual or imperfect flowers that have either one or the other. Perfect plants are more prone to self-pollination. Some have evolved devices to encourage cross- rather than self-pollination, and so boost the creation of the new genetic combinations that are the raw material for natural selection. So, sperm from a different baobab tree seems to travel faster down a style than does that from the same tree.

Flowering is the curtain-raiser to the main act of seed production, and its timing is critical. Near the tropics, where seasons are distinct, lengthening days or warmer temperatures may provide the necessary stimuli, and the appearance of leaves in October or November, and flowers shortly thereafter, is predictable. On the equator, seasonal temperatures vary less, and day lengths are constant enough for the Swahili clock to measure time by 12 hours of day and 12 of night all year round. There, more obscure environmental signals trigger the appearance of the great white blooms, which usually begin to show before the rains begin. They often appear before the leaves have started budding, when not only the baobabs, but almost every other tree around them, are bare-branched, and the entire grey-brown landscape anticipates rain.

Occasional flowers may appear at almost any time in the tree's annual cycle. In Mali, at

sepals with a velvety texture. When the flower is about to open, the calyx splits into sepals, which curve outwards to reveal five (occasionally four or six) crinkly white petals. The sepals unfold in a smooth, slow motion, and the flower takes less than half an hour to reach its full flamboyance.

Within the petals is an orb of hundreds of stamens, each tipped with an anther that produces pollen. Through the cluster of stamens protrudes the much longer style, ending in the stigma, the receptive end of the female reproductive organ.

the end of April, the lightning storms along the Bandiagara Escarpment in Dogon country can be spectacular – forks, sheets and flashes in an almost continuous two-hour show of *lumière* without the *son*. The storms are dry too, and the wind that follows brings only sand, not moisture. The year I visited, every baobab tree was still, nearly moribund, and absolutely bare, almost as if reluctant to risk flowering in that parched countryside until rain actually started falling.

The highlight of the day's walk to Tireli was the crocodile pool, where saurian relics of the last Ice Age were still said to linger, hundreds of desiccated semi-desert miles from their nearest fellows. That they sometimes did was clear from the little dead one at the mouth of a hole, but the pool was dusty dry, and we were told its inhabitants had retreated into spring-fed holes high up the cliffs. Near the pool stood a group of baobabs, all as bare as each other – except for one. On a low branch, within stretching distance, was a single glorious flower.

The one-night chance for that Malian flower to lure a nocturnal pollinator was over, and its unblemished petals suggested it had failed in nature's purpose. Soon its redundant corolla of discarded petals would slide down the style and drop to the ground, like millions of others are doing somewhere, most African mornings. Almost as if scorched by the sun's rays, the flowers would soon start to crumple, turning first a dirty brown, then a deep russet red.

Flowering before the rains start is risky. The advantage of doing so lies in being able to tempt pollinators with food in dry weather when there is little else to choose from. However, if the rains fail there may not be enough water to sustain seed growth, although this is less hazardous for baobabs, which store large amounts of water in their trunks, than it is for, say, acacias.

Baobabs in Kenya are divided into two distinct populations. At the coast most flower just before the long rains in April or May, bursting into leaf soon thereafter. Inland, some hormonal signal stimulates baobabs into blooming by the time the short rains start in October. Maverick trees in either population often operate on their own biological clock, flowering long before all the other baobabs around them, or coming into leaf when none of the others are.

Baobab flowers are open for about 18 hours – the arboreal equivalent of *Ephemera* mayflies – and for most of that time it is dark. Belying their beauty, they have an acrid smell that hints at something rotten, although there seems to be no English word that readily describes the smell, nor any with which it can easily be compared. Writers clutch at sensory straws in describing it as 'cabbagey' or 'like sour watermelon, urine, mice or sweaty feet'. None of the several authors of popular botanical books describing baobab flowers as 'sweetly scented' can ever have smelt them. Perhaps they have been beguiled by the magnificence of the photographed flower into believing it cannot be other than exquisitely perfumed.

Doyens of South African dendrology, Fried and Jutta von Breitenbach, camped under a baobab tree near the Zimbabwe border for four weeks in November 1972. They published their observations in the April–June 1974 issue of *Trees in South Africa*. The tree was already in full leaf, and began flowering the day they arrived, continuing to do so until just before they left.

Each evening the first buds started to crack around 6:30 pm, and within 20 minutes the sepals had curled back to reveal the mass of petals. These then unfolded to release the ball of stamens through which protruded the style. During the night the petals lifted still higher, like wings, further exposing the stamens to the attentions of nocturnal visitors. The next morning the process went into reverse, the closing sepals pressing the darkening petals back around the stamens, the whole tired and wilted flower then sliding down the style to the ground.

Pollination

Flowers evolve to balance the energy cost of blooming for a given length of time against the likelihood of receiving a visit from a pollinator while they are receptive. Pollination is a hit and miss affair at the best of times, one of nature's particularly chancy strategies. Where pollinators are scarce, or only visit flowers sporadically each day, as in temperate climates, flowers help their reproductive prospects by staying open much longer than they do near the equator. There, prolific bird, animal and insect life mean baobab flowers can open for just a few hours and still have a good chance of attracting pollinators.

Bats are either frugivorous or insectivorous, and it took a long time before botanists could say, with some scientific certainty, that they were the African baobab's prime pollinator. Bat pollination (chiropterophily) is unusual, and trees so pollinated show a number of distinctive design features. The flowers need to open at night, and must appeal more to a bat's olfactory senses than to its less efficient sense of sight. This sense of smell responds to odours that seem unappealing to humans, like the acrid scent of a baobab flower, which may have evolved to resemble that

Most of these flowers will have fallen off by the time new ones start opening in the evening.

of a bat. Bat-pollinated flowers should also be robust enough to allow the mammals to cling onto petals or stamens while eating pollen or lapping up nectar – of which these flowers usually produce large amounts. Crucially, the flowers must also be easy for bats to reach, growing on the ends of branches or long stalks so the visitors can easily swoop down in the dark without becoming entangled in twigs and leaves. The flowers of all other species of baobab grow on much shorter stalks, protruding either erectly or horizontally off the branches. Such orientation is ill-suited to bat pollination and the blooms rely on birds and insects to spread their pollen.

Sausage trees (*Kigelia africana*) often grow in the same parts of Africa as do baobabs. Not only do these trees share the obvious characteristic of producing big, heavy fruit, both are also bat-pollinated. The sausage tree's exquisite crimson flowers have a smell that is also very unappealing to humans. They hang down off stalks that are anything from 2 to 7 m long, around which bats can easily flutter.

Bat pollination is a tropical phenomenon generally, and in Africa many of the bats that sip baobab or sausage tree nectar do so largely because there is no fruit around when these trees are flowering. Two particular species of fruit bat are identified as frequent baobab pollinators. One is the straw-coloured fruit bat that often roosts colonially in town parks. The other is the Egyptian fruit bat, which has evolved a simple echolocation system, unusual for fruit bats, but typical for the cave-rooster that it is. As lots of

Fruit bats love figs, like these of *Ficus bussei*, taking them away to eat elsewhere. Ironically, in the course of pollinating baobabs, bats may drop fig seeds into the hollows of forked branches; these seeds may germinate, ultimately condemning the baobab to death.

Bushbabies or galagos (here, a lesser galago) are occasional pollinators of baobab flowers.

bats appeared. It was bewitching to watch them scrabbling and twittering around the tree, backed by the rising moon's reflection in the silvery-black sea. They would swoop down onto the outlying branches – the flowers were unrecognizable as such in the dark – cling on with flapping wings for just a few seconds, then fall away and flit off to find more nectar.

Individual baobab trees are usually sparing with their blooms each night, and few flowers open at once. This prompts bats to move from tree to tree – so promoting cross-pollination – rather than to feast on a single tree and merely move pollen from one of its flowers to another. By the staggered flowering of trees in the same population, and at least a few flowers on any single tree opening every night for up to six weeks, the supply of baobab nectar is effectively prolonged, and pollinators kept interested enough to return. The tree observed by the Von Breitenbachs produced about 400 flowers over the course of four weeks.

bats roosting together quickly exhaust nearby food supplies, they need to forage far from their home cave or grove of trees. Baobabs growing a long way from roosts, therefore, still have good chances of attracting passing bats with their pungent flowers.

On the south coast of Kenya is the small fishing village of Msambweni, which lends its name to four kilometres of nearby beach. At one end of the beach the sand gives way to a rocky headland of fossilized coral, beyond which is a jumble of cracks, caves and chimneys that make an ideal roost for bats. Thousands of bats, mostly Egyptian fruit bats, emerge in the early evening before heading up or down the coast to feed.

At the other end of Msambweni beach, close to the village, is a beautiful grove of baobabs on the edge of a football pitch. When I visited there one December at twilight, a single baobab was in full flower. Within minutes of my arrival, 20 or 30

This hawkmoth is 'feeding for free', extracting nectar without making contact with the reproductive parts of the flower of *Adansonia za* in Madagascar.

The petals and stamens have slipped down the style to the ground. If pollination has been successful the ovary will soon start to enlarge.

Bats leave clear evidence of their nocturnal visits to baobab flowers in the claw marks on the petals, which are already dark-edged the next morning. Baobab petals are particularly rich in tannin. This oxidizes very quickly, turning the whole petal brown in a few hours. The fallen petals are resilient, and remain easily recognizable as recent components of baobab flowers, even after being rained upon. Slowly, they dry out into brittle chestnut crisps that litter the earth around the trees for many weeks after falling.

Bushbabies have also been observed pollinating baobabs while munching petals or sipping nectar. They may be locally effective pollinators, but in the greater scheme of things they are too few, and too sparsely distributed, to do more than act as occasional

The enormous variation in both shape and size of fruit has given taxonomists reason to think there may be several subspecies of *Adansonia digitata*. These particularly large fruit come from trees near Kilifi on the Kenyan coast.

agents of pollen transfer. Like most mammals that don't fly, they make poor cross-pollinators, and if they move pollen from the stamens of one flower to the stigma of another it is most likely to be between flowers on the same tree.

Giant carpenter bees crawl all over the orb of stamens, honey bees clamber more delicately over the flower, collecting pollen, ants rush around the petals and even bluebottles seem to be attracted by the rotting smell of fading flowers. These insects may be gathering pollen, or may inadvertently collect it on their bodies. However, they usually move on without leaving any on the flower's style, which protrudes so far beyond the stamens that insects seldom come in contact with its tip.

Seed pods

Young seed pods look like large green or browny-green plums, then apples, before taking on more familiar cucumber, marrow or melon shapes. Starting off pale green, they slowly darken and harden, becoming more grey or yellow. Stalk lengths differ too, seeming to vary with the size of the fruit they support.

There are some spectacular baobabs in northeastern Namibia, near Tsumkwe, including the Grootboom ('big tree' in Afrikaans), which is surrounded by several smaller trees. When I visited one August, one of these attendants had distinctly pink bark, quite different in colour from the other grey-trunked trees. To add strength to the contention that differently coloured baobabs may be genetically distinct, the fruit of the pink Namibian tree was elongated, in obvious contrast to the spherical baubles dangling off the other baobabs.

Among hundreds of trees around Kilifi on the Kenyan coast, after a long rainy season was easing off into scattered July squalls, most pods were like huge fat marrows, but there were some distinct oddities among them. Some trees had grown fruit

These petals and stamens have caught on the end of the style and will remain there as the fruit continues to ripen.

contoured somewhere between a giant comma and a human foetus – quite like expanded versions of the kidney-shaped seeds within them. Another tree was losing its greenery long before most of the others, giving it a sickly look by comparison with its lustrous neighbours. Among its remaining leaves hung seed pods shaped like cylindrical balloons, each with a small unfilled nipple at the end, tipped with the remnants of the wizened style.

Internally, pods are divided lengthways into sections by the coarse brown fibres that have channelled nourishment to growing seeds. Within each section seeds nestle comfortably into the vitamin C-rich pith that supports them. Seeds are not easily parted from their pith, but, once they are, appear as dark brown kidney beans, about a centimetre long, with soft, nutty-tasting centres.

Most pods lie where they fall and are quickly invaded by ants, Heteroptera bugs and other insects.

Seed dispersal

Any seed pod's contents are far more useful to the species when spread away from the plant that produced them. Many big trees have vast splaying webs of roots, so that even if seeds germinated where they fell, they could scarcely survive to compete with their parent. Nature provides external agents to disperse seeds, either in the random form of wind, water or passing creatures, or in the deliberate actions of animals eating seeds, which they expel elsewhere. Seeds are often coated with fruit, which acts as an inducement to birds or animals to swallow them, the journey through digestive systems ultimately helping them germinate.

Botanically speaking, pods are described as 'indehiscent', meaning they do not open spontaneously while still on the tree. (One of the characteristics of the Australian boab, distinguishing it from all other species in the genus, is that pods crack open before they fall.) The fruit of *Adansonia digitata* may hang on the tree for a very long time, yet no matter how reluctant the tree is to let them go, they never open on the branches.

Fallen pods usually remain intact when they drop, slowly drying out and their shells becoming brittle. Then rot sets in and, by the time the next crop of pods is ripe, all that remains of the previous year's fruit are scattered fragments of shell.

Large pods may weigh over 2 kg and contain more than 400 seeds – the most I have counted in Kenya was 462. These are super-fruit compared to pods in drier parts of Africa, where seed numbers in tiny, apple-sized pods may not reach double figures. If the pods lie where they land, the rotting shells are soon invaded by ants, termites and brightly coloured cotton-stainer bugs, bringing in soil and moisture. Crush a fallen pod, and it is often already full of the damp earth that provides such an ideal environment for seed germination.

Did these small trunks grow out of fallen seeds of the parent tree, or are they offshoots from its tap root?

Baboons either feast up in the tree, pulling fruit off the branches, or carry pods off and crack them open in solitary peace some distance away.

Monkeys love the pith in baobab pods – the vitamin-rich coating on the indigestible pill. It takes the jaws of a baboon to break open a big baobab fruit, and smaller monkeys may have to make do with fallen, weaker-shelled pods. Baboons invade fruiting baobabs with the enthusiasm of locusts for a field of greenery. One April I found nearly 50 of them adorning almost the only tree in Tanzania's Tarangire National Park, which was leafless and in fruit. Baboons are noisy creatures and seem compelled to accompany every activity with snarls and screams, sounding far more vicious than they really are. Yet this pith must be the manna that sustains them in their wilderness,

ABOVE: This baobab had two particular attractions for baboons: it was the only tree in fruit for kilometres around, and the baboons were able to reach its branches by first climbing the adjacent thorn tree.

Hanging over the waters
of the Indian Ocean on
a tiny coral outcrop near
the Kenya–Somali border,
this tree must surely have
emerged from a seed that
was dispersed by the sea.

Baobab seeds are still easily recognizable after passing through the digestive system of a baboon, and are more likely to germinate having done so.

and with concentration that left no room for bickering, they would pull a pod off a branch and crack it open in their jaws. Then they picked away at the contents with their hands, just like their human relations dipping into packets of crisps. The only sound from the tree was the drip, drip, of discarded bits of shell, hitting the ground with a staccato rhythm of raindrops falling off the leaves after a passing storm.

Baobab trunks are often too smooth for baboons to climb, but these monkeys started gingerly down the trunk, tail first, and then leapt onto a nearby acacia tree, which they descended with ease. Once on *terra firma* they behaved in more conventional baboon fashion, scrapping over fallen fruit and aggressively preserving their pecking order. Often they would scamper off onto the rocky slopes nearby, a seed pod in their jaws, there to eat quietly on their own, away from the frenzy of communal baboon existence. Baboons are after the pith, and sometimes frustrate nature's design by spitting out the seeds. Usually though, they eat the entire contents of the pod, and in this

way seeds reach the stony areas where the baboons like to rest, and where young seedlings have a better chance of not being eaten by livestock or trampled by large game animals.

Swallowed seeds are easily identifiable in baboon droppings. Walking up the edge of the Athi River in Tsavo National Park, I came to a patch of sand where a party of baboons had obviously rested, lots of bean-shaped baobab seeds showing clearly in their droppings. All the trees I had seen so far were without pods and leaves, but this meant a nearby one must be in fruit, and, as if to confirm this, near another pile of droppings were scattered pieces of pod shell. I could not see the tree until I was well away from the river, and not before first finding more bits of shell, the attached fibres still bright chestnut. The pods had recently been opened and canine teeth marks showed clearly. The baboons had been eating fallen fruit, rather than climbing the tree to feast. Fruit ripped straight off branches comes away with twigs and strips of bark, whereas withered stalks were still attached to these pods, showing them to have ripened and fallen naturally.

The bright chestnut fibres are a clear sign of fresh fruit having been recently opened by baboons.

The Kunene River in full flood probably deposited the seeds from which these trees grew.

Where baboons are scarce, baobab seeds will not get the transport to distant cliffs or rocky kopjes so crucial to the species' future. Today's arable farmers cannot afford baboons rampaging through their crops, and the monkeys' dwindling numbers must inevitably bring about a shrinkage in the range of the tree. One of many possible reasons for the very restricted distribution of Madagascar's baobabs may be their having evolved to rely for dispersal of their seeds on the appetites of elephant birds or giant lemurs, both of which are now extinct.

Elephants may eat whole pods, or their contents, although reports of their doing so are scarce, and most focus their, often destructive, energies on the trees' trunks. Mice, rats, squirrels and other small mammals certainly contribute to the dispersal of baobab seeds, at least beyond the tree canopy where they fall. Water also carries baobab pods down rivers and round lake shores, but not to the same extent it disperses the seeds of doum palms or coconuts.

Baobabs growing on islands in the middle of wide African rivers are unquestionably spread by water. The Kunene River originates in the highlands of Angola, and its lower reaches form the boundary with Namibia. The Epupa Falls are the visual high point of this river's journey to the sea. Between the tumble of different cataracts are tiny rocky islets, to many of which small baobabs cling – among the best-watered specimens on the continent.

Baobabs live to great ages. In their early years fruit will be small and few, increasing in size and number as the trunk thickens and branches lengthen. Perhaps an average baobab fruits first aged 30, and then once a year for the next 200 years. And perhaps it produces between 20 and 500 pods every time it bears fruit, with an average of 300 every year over those 200 years. Each of

these pods contains a dry-country average of 100 seeds – an average total of 30 000 seeds each year for 200 years, making a lifetime's output of six million. (A single common oak (*Quercus robur*) has been estimated to produce five million acorns in what may be a similar lifespan.)

To keep any population of mature baobabs, or oaks, at its present level, each specimen needs to produce one offspring that survives to fruit by the time its parent dies. So, one mature tree needs to grow from the six million seeds produced by an average baobab during an average lifespan. Numbers of seeds might naturally seem to affect numbers of trees, but this vast surplus makes the connection extremely tenuous. Most seeds

never germinate, either failing to attract the attentions of a dispersal agent or falling on the proverbial stony ground, even if they do. Others will germinate and start to shoot, synthesizing water and carbon dioxide into nourishment for herbivorous mammals.

While producing baobab seeds by the million may seem wasteful from a baobab perspective, either they, or the seedlings they produce, serve to nourish the multitudes of other creatures living in baobab country; otherwise they rot away, fertilizing the ground around the tree that produced them. Indeed, it is as well that baobabs, or any other naturally occurring species, are not too successful. If, during their lives, each

breeding baobab produced even five saplings that survived to maturity, after two generations there would be 25 times as many baobabs smothering the savanna. This may be fine for baobabs but the population explosion could only be bought at the price of driving out many other plants from the savanna mosaic – and bringing us one step closer to turning into reality the alarming scenario in Antoine de Saint-Exupery's *Le Petit Prince* – that 'if the planet is too small, and if the baobabs are too numerous, they will finally make the planet explode'.

PREVIOUS PAGES AND BELOW: The majority of seeds from most fruits will never germinate.

CHAPTER FOUR

Life and death

It is tough for a tree trying to gain a roothold on the open plains of the savanna, or the flatlands of fossilized coral along the coastline. Scarcely any part of Africa is left ungrazed by wild game or herds of domestic livestock. Being protected by neither thorns nor a foul taste, baobab shoots are prime food. Human populations outside national parks and wildlife reserves are rising dramatically, often straining the environment to the limit. Inside these protected areas grazing pressures are often just as intense, now that wild animals find it increasingly difficult to make seasonal migrations in and out of them.

Emerging life

The coat of a baobab seed is hard and water-resistant, and several hours among the acidic waste of a baboon's digestive system will not only soften the seed coat, but also kill off any insects that might otherwise have damaged seeds. Emerging along with an immediate supply of natural fertilizer has its advantages too. Fire helps break the dormancy of seeds, and charring the exocarps of the baobabs may also help shoots break out. Having done so, a succession of well-spaced tropical thunderstorms, with hot drying days in between, will help seeds germinate.

Good years for baobab seedlings are most likely good years for other plants as well. Young baobabs may, therefore, be smothered before they get a chance to penetrate the tangle of surrounding vegetation, starved of life-giving light, water or nourishment. If they do survive among the competition in their first, most fragile months, they still need to be well watered over the next few years before they are strong enough to withstand the long dry spells that typify much of their range.

To try and add some simple science to the common sense, let me take the hypothesis of the average baobab in the previous chapter one step further. Very roughly, if 5% of the tree's annual seed crop of 30 000 eventually germinates and, of those, 5% live to the following year, there will be 75 saplings. In order to maintain the population at existing levels, at least one of those 75 trees must survive the rigours of baobab life long enough to start reproducing.

With each passing year the fast-growing tree gains strength, more resistance to drought, greater chances of surviving loss of leaves to hungry goats or impala – and more flexibility to withstand trampling by cattle or Cape buffalo. Fire remains a potent danger to growing trees long after they are too big to be flattened by passing mammals.

While mature baobabs are little affected by bush fires raging around their trunks, several years of saplings can be destroyed in a single blaze, particularly if grass is long and flames burn hot. Ironically, the same fire that can devastate the young baobabs may also help break the dormancy of the next crop of seeds. And, still more ironically, mature baobabs may even conduct the lightning that starts the fire that burns their offspring.

In those parts of Africa blessed with two rainy seasons, baobabs grow much faster than they do where they have to rely on two consecutive months of scattered downpours. Young trees are measured by height rather than girth, and in well-watered country may be a metre tall after two years and 10 m after 20. In areas of semi-desert, like the Sahel and southern Sudan, any trees that escape the feet and mouths of hungry livestock, as well as droughts and fires, grow much slower. Always, the seeds with the best chances of maturing into small trees are those that germinate on a rocky hillside, although these will only grow very slowly.

PREVIOUS PAGES: Next to this baobab on Botswana's Lekhubu Island, a dead one decomposes among the rocks.
BELOW: The living and the near-dead – a single branch grows out of the stump of a fallen tree.

Young baobabs often go unnoticed, not least because their leaves are so different from those of mature trees.

Cryptic beginnings

The tiny, new trees are quite unrecognizable as would-be baobabs. Instead of the finger-like leaves of mature trees, young baobabs have simple, elliptical ones, successfully concealing their identity from all but the most dedicated searcher. Saplings' leaves are paired, one opposite the other, with the next pair appearing at right angles to the ones below. As they grow, little trees produce more baobab-like leaves with three indistinct points, but these still do not resemble the compound, digitate foliage from which the species takes its name.

In the first two or three years, young trees have a shrubby look, their limbs protruding horizontally. Thereafter, the branches start reaching upwards, rather than outwards, giving the tree an odd enough look to invite a second glance. One hundred and fifty years ago Thomas Baines

described young boabs in Australia as resembling a champagne bottle with a branching twig stuck in its cork. With age, baobabs of the African species begin conforming to that description too, by which time they may be designated 'pachycauls', meaning thick-stemmed.

Baobab trees are usually grey or grey-brown, elephant coloured, sometimes with a red or purple tinge to them. On the mystical granite outcrop of Lekhubu Island in northern Botswana, baobabs frame the vistas out over the ancient lake bed of what is now the Sua Pan to an unbroken horizon. Some are a deep copper colour, as if chemically tainted by the alkaline soil below, others have a golden sheen to their trunks, and a few are pink on the upper surfaces of their branches, almost looking sunburnt. Not far away are the famous 'Baines Boababs', so called because Thomas Baines made a watercolour painting of them in 1862. Struggling to get the colours right, he notes in his diary entry for 21 May that:

The general colour of the immense stems was grey and rough; but where the old bark had peeled and curled off, the new (of that peculiar metallic coppery-looking red and yellow which Dr. Livingstone was wont so strenuously to object to in my pictures) shone through over large portions, giving them, according to light or shade, a red or yellow grey or a deep purple tone.'

Bark can be smooth and shiny, giving trees a lustrous aura of good health. Comparisons to human skin and the body it encases are inescapable. The surface of old trees becomes crinkled and wrinkled, or pitted with arboreal scars. Sometimes the woody matter is bunched

This pink-barked tree in Namibia was growing close to others with more normal coloured trunks, suggesting that bark colour is not affected by minerals in the soil.

like dripping candle wax or rolls of fat, branches splaying out like waving arms. Trunks are often covered with nodules, dense enough to remind one of the knobbly stems of the baobab's Brazilian bombax relative. The bark can have the matt look of stone, too, and when bits of trunk spread over slabs of rock it may require touch to distinguish one from the other.

Just below the outer bark is a layer of bright green, easily exposed by scratching with fingernails. This is chlorophyll, thought to help the tree photosynthesize during long leafless periods, without losing water. Species of the *Commiphora* genus can probably also absorb solar energy through their trunks and branches, vividly coloured in different shades of bright green or blue beneath the peeling, papery bark.

Injured trees usually heal when bark from the wound edges grows inwards to cover the bare patches, just as cuts on human skin mend. Baobab bark is remarkable for its spectacular ability to regenerate directly out of the wood of the tree, although early scars linger into later life. Such resilience is one of the reasons why the trees are able to survive massive damage to bark and wood by thirsty, mineral-hungry elephants. These regenerative powers also have a profound effect on the tree's physiognomy. They allow trunks and branches to bend, crack and splinter, the wounds then healing so completely that the tree looks as if the contorted shape actually results from natural growth rather than well-mended injury.

Leaves and water

On the twig ends are digitate leaves, usually five-, but sometimes four-, six- or seven-fingered (leaves of all counts even growing on the same branch). The baobab in full foliage is a splendid sight, towering high and dark above the surrounding vegetation. The stark silhouette of the dry months

is now softened by the luxuriant mass of greenery.

This magnificent canopy maximizes the opportunities for photosynthesis – that utterly fundamental of all biological processes and the basis of almost all other forms of life. Baobabs present hundreds of thousands of broad, chlorophyll-laden blades to the sun, and, with the aid of this solar energy, turn huge amounts of carbon dioxide and water into sugar and oxygen. Like most trees growing out in the open, rather than in dense forest, baobabs have rounded hemispherical crowns that maximize the trees'

Commiphora species are leafless for most of the year and so photosynthesize through their trunks, as baobabs are also thought to do.

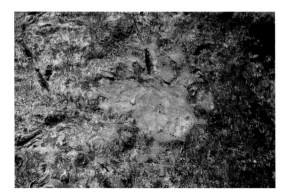

Just underneath the baobab's grey surface is a thin layer of bright green bark, which may help sustain photosynthetic activity when the tree is leafless.

Despite the species name, *digitata*, six or seven, rather than five, leaflets often make up a single leaf.

exposure to sunlight and minimize the shading of one layer of leaves by another. The digitate configuration of the leaves also lets sunlight filter in between the leaflets.

The price for such massive photosynthetic activity, however, is colossal loss of water through transpiration. The undersides of leaves are covered in holes (stomata), through which carbon dioxide is absorbed, and oxygen and water emitted. Leaves of mature baobabs are far larger than those of most trees growing in the dry African bush, and so allow the loss of much more water than do leaves of other trees.

Being in leaf during the rainy season gives baobabs the best chance to replenish water lost in transpiration by continually drawing up more through their roots. To minimize water loss, baobabs have an annual cycle that has them in full leaf for about four months before the tree begins absorbing nutrients from the leaves. As it does, the green chlorophyll, which masked other pigments, begins to disappear, and carotene and xanthophyll dominate the leaf colour with oranges and yellows. When the leaflets start falling, they are finally tinged by the tannin a lingering autumnal brown.

Besides keeping their leaves for such a short time, boababs have evolved another aid to survival, and store huge amounts of water in their wood. This high water content is not immediately

The rounded crown of a baobab maximizes the exposure of its leaves to sunlight and, therefore, the tree's photosynthetic activity.

obvious, and certainly doesn't make the tree any softer to the touch. Yet for all its unyielding rigidity, there is enough water in the wood to provoke debate on whether the baobab actually qualifies as a succulent.

A question of succulence

In Volume 36 of the *Cactus and Succulent Journal of Great Britain* (1974), Len Newton, Professor of Botany at Nairobi University, posited the question 'Is the Baobab Tree Succulent?', concluding that 'it depends on what you mean by succulent'. In the absence of a universally accepted definition of a succulent this actually seems a logical, if unsatisfactory, end to the argument. Bruce

Hargreaves of Botswana's National Museum defines succulents in the broadest terms as 'plants which store water' and so has no hesitation in including *Adansonia digitata* in *The Succulents of Botswana*. Plants can store water in trunks as well as leaves, and if stem-succulents are accepted into the lists, baobabs are inescapably due for inclusion. Their trunks are water laden in the extreme even without a fleshy consistency, as are those of desert roses (*Adenium obesum*). Those arguing that baobabs are succulents will be comforted by their appearance in both the three-volume *Handbook of Succulent Plants* by Hermann Jacobson of Kiel Botanical Gardens, and in B P Barkhuizen's *Succulents of Southern Africa*.

Water content is best measured by comparing the weight of recently cut timber against that of air-dried wood. Freshly felled baobab trunks weigh around 840 kg per cubic metre – although clearly weight changes with the season. Air drying, when most water is extracted from the wood, brings this down to around 200 kg per cubic metre. These figures make baobabs only slightly more watery than human beings, but much less so than Saguaro cacti (*Carnegiea gigantea*) of Hollywood horizons and the Arizona desert. These are the largest cacti on Earth, also, incidentally, pollinated by bats, and 90% water after a good storm. Like baobabs, they have a far-reaching web of shallow roots to maximize absorption of moisture, but unlike baobabs they have no leaves through which to lose water, photosynthesizing entirely through their trunks.

Desert roses and baobabs often grow in the same dry environments and have both evolved to store large quantities of water in their trunks.

Baobabs actually rely on water to keep them upright. The liquid creates the hydraulic pressure that maintains the trees in their distended, water-logged state. Saguaro cacti store water as a jelly in their tissue. Although they can lose up to 80% of this moisture, thick waxy skin acts as a sort of supporting ecto-skeleton and also prevents complete dehydration. Baobabs' water loss is less extreme, but during very dry times their girths can still contract.

For such a prodigious hydraulic intake, a baobab needs an extensive web of roots. The tree's first major root is a tap root that heads straight down into the soil, before ballooning out just below the surface as the trunk begins expanding. When baobabs fall over, this bulbous mass of solid root wood may be pulled out of the ground by the weight of the trunk, leaving a deep wide hole, like a tooth extracted from its gum. An old tree's root mass may start rotting at the same time as the heartwood in the trunk, and the tree gradually hollows both above and below the ground.

A tree's root system is usually far closer to the surface than popularly supposed. The exposed silhouette of roots and tree may be compared to that of a wine glass, with the roots forming the flat base to the stem of the trunk. Huge baobab roots are often partly exposed above the ground, either because they are spreading out over rocks or because the soil that once covered them has eroded. One of the roots of Chapman's Baobab shows above the soil 65 m from the trunk, still as thick as a bloated python.

With such huge trunks, and often having to gather a year's supply of water from occasional storms within a few weeks, the web of a baobab's roots spreads far wider than that of many other trees. In Senegal, Michel Adanson not only measured the circumference of the trees, but also examined the roots:

> '… my guide led me to a second, which was
> sixty-three feet in circumference, … and one of
> its roots, which had been for the most part laid bare
> by a neighbouring river, was a hundred and ten feet
> in length, without reckoning the part that lay hid
> under the water, and which I could not uncover.'

Hardwood pegs are easy to hammer into the soft, water-laden tissue of the baobab's trunk. Here a Hadzabe honey hunter makes a ladder up a tree.

Various attempts have been made to devise formulae to calculate the span of baobab roots – two or three times the radius of the branches or so many times the height of the tree. Generally, baobab bulk, and thus water requirement, is related less to height than to girth; this would therefore seem a more appropriate measurement with which to link root length. In the course of my researches I explored the root systems of many baobabs and, if forced to devise a formula for root length, it would be just under three times tree height.

The high water content of their wood has contrary consequences for baobabs. Elephants attack them mercilessly in times of drought, obtaining water or minerals by gouging wood out of the trunk to the point of its collapse. Yet this same waterlogged state makes the wood very difficult to burn, and saves trees from much human destruction. It also makes them extremely awkward to fell. During the abortive Ground Nut Scheme in Tanzania – when millions of acres of virgin Tanzanian bush were cleared after World War II to make way for oil-producing peanuts – bulldozers, army tanks, and even dynamite, failed to shift the bigger baobabs.

A distinctive outline

The core, the character, the essence of the baobab is its shape, size and silhouette. Baobabs need thick twigs to support large heavy leaves, giving branch ends the stumpy look of fingers clawing at the sky, as if these terminal twigs had stopped

This baobab is being transplanted and shows the thick tap root that young trees soon develop.

As they fatten and contort, trunks and roots may clasp large rocks, which are eventually lifted off the ground.

short of further bifurcations. The branches of species with smaller leaves divide into much more spindly twigs, giving such trees a much fuzzier look from a distance.

The combination of trunk and branches confers on each baobab its own distinctive outline. One characteristic of many baobabs is that they divide, low down, into two or more boles. Sometimes these remain almost as one, encased by the same bark and probably functioning as a single part of the tree. Other boles split away from each other, so close to the ground that they could almost have emerged from different seeds. Whether they did or not is impossible to

prove, although DNA analysis might confirm the unlikely event of their having germinated from seeds of different trees. That two trunks can emerge from the same seed is beyond doubt; all three tiny trees in my Nairobi garden have grown second stems, perhaps regrowth from insect damage at the top of the tap root.

Some trees retain a bottle shape from immaturity through to old age. The trunk fills out, developing either a long central tapering top, or otherwise a cluster of waving arm-like branches. Others may not fatten out to the same extent, but still produce branches continuing straight up out of the trunk, as if the tree had been pollarded and the limbs were growing again. More often, at least some branches grow out sideways and, if the tree lives long enough, these begin to sag under the twin burdens of annual crops of heavy fruit and their own water-laden weight.

Trunks and branches may dip so low they touch the ground. One of the trunks of the famous Dorsland Tree, near Tsumkwe in Namibia, seems to have succumbed under the burden of its own history, and all else it has carried over the past several hundred years. Now bending down to the ground, the relief of no longer having to support itself seems to have given the trunk a new life of its own, and tangles of young branches are thrusting their way skywards once more.

It is wrong to invest these different forms with too much significance. There seems little, if any, correlation between tree shape and distribution. Rather, the myriad variation in the configuration of trunks and branches is yet another aspect of what makes the trees so intriguing, non-conformist, and individual. A tree's final shape can also be affected by incidents in early life. Having the leafy top munched off by a hungry elephant, as a sapling, will almost certainly influence the outline of the mature tree; so will the unwanted attentions of the larvae of Cerambycidae beetles, boring their way around inside the stems of growing trees.

Elephant damage to older trees provides a wonderful glimpse into the otherwise hidden secrets of a baobab's trunk, and an early chance to see if it is hollow. Older trees of many species are hollow long before they die, and such hollowness

Did these trunks grow from one seed or two? Even if they grew from two, the seeds probably derived from the same parent tree, and genetic analysis may not even distinguish them.

Elephants have dug away at both sides of this baobab's trunk, revealing its hollowness and giving a view right through to another tree in the distance.

after another, they are gradually relegated from live, functioning sapwood, to solid, yet redundant, heartwood. Gums and resins often give heartwood a different texture or colour. Being dead and contributing nothing to the workings of the tree, heartwood's principal function might seem one of structural support. Yet a tree's slowly decaying centre may also provide it with a vital source of food, prolonging life by hundreds more years. New feeder roots may even grow down to suck out goodness from the rotting balloon of root material below a disintegrating trunk.

Branches often break off baobabs in their prime, the mass of fruit- or leaf-laden, waterlogged wood finally succumbing to the forces of gravity. Sometimes one broken branch or trunk leaves others unsupported and they soon follow it earthwards, the whole finally resembling a gigantic half-peeled, half-eaten banana.

Eventually the stress of maintaining such a huge trunk, hollow or not, and all its branches, will prove too much for the root system. Disease, like the fungal affliction called sooty baobab disease, which was particularly apparent in Zimbabwe during the 1980s, may then invade the tree's fragile state. Otherwise drought takes its toll, perhaps compounded by moisture loss from the soil as surrounding ground cover is overgrazed. Weakened trees that have previously withstood frequent frosts succumb to temperatures no lower than they have endured for hundreds of years before.

Exactly how a tree collapses depends very much on its shape. Bottle-shaped trees with thick trunks and much thinner branches are more likely to lose those branches than to fall over. On more cylindrical trees, branches spreading horizontally away from the trunk may snap off, or their weight eventually exert so much leverage on the trunk that roots no longer provide a strong enough anchor to keep it on the ground.

seems to cause no immediate ill effects. Living longer, and containing more water than most other species, baobabs are particularly inclined to hollowness, although it must be unusual for trees only 85 years old to respond to knocks on their trunks with that sound of nothing in the middle – as do both specimens in the Nairobi Arboretum.

Death

Trees lengthen by growing new wood onto the tips of their branches, and widen by adding layers around their trunks. (Carved initials or pruning scars stay in roughly the same place on a tree all its life, but initials become increasingly hard to decipher.) As old layers get buried by one new one

Toppling over may or may not signal the death of the tree. That same elasticity, derived from its waterlogged wood, makes roots bend rather than snap, and many near-horizontal trunks retain at least some contact with their source of nutrients and water. New shoots often sprout out of these fallen trees, like independent bushes. Round the bottom of the upended trunk, an outer layer of protective cambium may grow over the jagged fractures of snapped roots, just as it seals scars of broken branches.

Baobabs are known to live for many more years in a supine state. Among the many reasons for the notoriety of the Baines Baobabs in Botswana can be added the resilience of one sleeping giant.

In his diary entry Baines describes how:

'A long circuit brought me ...
to the clump of baobabs we had
seen yesterday from the wagon; five full-
sized trees and two or three younger ones
were standing, so that when in leaf their
foliage must form one magnificent shade.
One gigantic trunk had fallen and
lay prostrate, but still losing none
if its vitality, sent forth branches
and young leaves like the rest.'

The tree retains its vitality today.

PREVIOUS PAGES: One huge branch breaking off a baobab tends to destroy the mutual support system that kept the whole tree together, and others soon follow.
ABOVE: This charred-looking Namibian baobab is in fact afflicted with a fungal infection called sooty baobab disease.

Trees have been said to be set alight spontaneously by both breaking branches or collapsing trunks. Yet such stories always seem to be at least second hand, and eyewitness accounts of these bizarre incidents are conspicuously lacking. Hollow baobabs are often blackened as a result of fires that were lit inside their trunks, when they served as homes or hideouts while the trees were still alive. Charred stumps of broken branches are sometimes signs that honey gatherers have been at work on bees' nests. These fire scars from the tree's earlier life could be wrongly attributed to its time of collapse. Once a large baobab trunk has fallen over or crumpled where it stands, the great mass of rotting, water-laden wood may easily start to smoulder and steam. Any of these scenarios could stir minds into fitting facts to the fancy of the myth rather than to a more prosaic reality.

Even when the last root snaps, and all contact with the ground has gone, there remains enough water in the bloated stem to fuel a few hopeful shoots for a few months. But the giant dehydrates quickly and begins crumbling where it lies, the heartwood so soft and damp one can pull off chunks or push fingers into it. Eventually, the whole baobab rots away, back into the ground from which it emerged. Perhaps among the richer vegetation that is nourished by the remains of the old tree is a young one, no longer held back by the towering presence of its parent and now able to gather nutrients from the fallen corpse.

With mountains eroding and lakes silting up, why should ancient baobabs

This family in Mtwara, southern Tanzania, was nearly crushed by the collapse of a baobab. They described it falling slowly earthwards early one evening 'as if sleeping'.

not assume the distinction of near-permanent fixtures? In one of the agreements, signed in 1900, whereby Britain and Germany sliced up the East African cake between them, baobabs were considered enduring enough features of the landscape to demarcate the Kenya–Tanganyika border:

> 'From this point the boundary follows N 70 E (astronomical) in a
> straight line to point No 5 (large baobab tree on the high part of the bank).
> On this line several mangrove poles have been planted …
> On the high bank the boundary goes from the baobab at No 5 past a second
> baobab to a third baobab. Two blocks of cement have been placed in the intervening
> space, and marks have been cut upon the baobabs. From the third baobab …'

Yet the baobabs disappointed. By 1993, less than 100 years later, no trace of any of them remained.

TOP LEFT: Despite having fallen over, this baobab's root system is clearly intact and is sending water and nutrients up to the three healthy new shoots.

TOP: The fallen tree that so intrigued Thomas Baines, and which is still sending out shoots every year, nearly 150 years later.

ABOVE: This fallen baobab had been used as a shelter. The remnants of fires inside were not a result of spontaneous combustion.

LEFT: Three huge trunks have collapsed in different directions; within a few years, the only sign that a baobab ever grew here will be relict clumps of invasive vegetation.

CHAPTER FIVE

How old? How big?

Big baobabs must be old. Can anything grow that huge without taking hundreds, if not thousands, of years to do so? However efficiently their root systems collect water, and no matter what devices they have evolved to limit moisture loss through leaves, given where they grow, big trees must be old trees. That is the voice of good sense, and the most profound science is not going to silence it. Small is certainly not necessarily young in the tree world, but big simply has to be old.

Ageing trees

And how old is old? Almost anyone with at least a passing interest in baobabs asks the question. The Prussian explorer Friedrich von Humboldt may only just have been exaggerating in calling baobabs the 'oldest organic monuments of our planet' and suggesting they 'would date back to the times of the Pyramid builders' (c. 2 500 BC).

Two hundred years ago, Von Humboldt, and other travellers with more fanciful than scientific bents, could make such unfounded assertions without challenge. Today, in the times of written history scattered with dates, chronologies and anniversaries, 'old' has become an increasingly inadequate description of either natural or man-made monuments. The age of everything, from the universe onwards, is questioned, investigated and, if possible, ascertained.

Knowing a tree's age does satisfy a certain curiosity, and perhaps enhances the sense of awe and wonder one feels in its presence. It also slots trees into a historical perspective, as

PREVIOUS SPREAD: If the Grootboom in Namibia is Africa's biggest baobab, it will be the continent's largest living organism. It is remarkable not only for its girth, but also its height.
ABOVE: No matter how abundant its water supply, this baobab at Lake Manyara in Tanzania must have taken hundreds of years to grow so large.

witnesses to passing history. Yet at the same time, answering the question 'how old' inevitably risks demystifying these ancient relics. Some may be content just to wonder if Jesus Christ actually prayed under some of the olive trees (*Olea eoropaea*) still growing in what is left of the Garden of Gethsemane, or if there is still an oak in Sherwood Forest which sheltered Robin Hood while he loved Maid Marion. Is it enough to ask if the baobabs at Malindi, on the Kenyan coast, are the very same ones that surely astounded Vasco da Gama?

Ageing ancient trees still remains a combination of science, practical good sense, guesswork and wishful thinking. Science's contribution comes largely from carbon dating, a notoriously arcane, and unreliable, way of ascertaining the age of any organic material. Radiocarbon (principally carbon-14) in molecules of carbon dioxide is continually absorbed by green plants from the atmosphere. Once a plant dies the process ceases, and the accumulated radiocarbon steadily declines. The rate of decline is expressed in terms of a half-life – the length of time that half the amount of radiocarbon takes to disappear. Carbon-14 has a half-life of around 5 700 years. The graph of radiocarbon decline is the same for any organism, so date of death can be estimated by assessing the amount of carbon remaining at the time of measurement.

Heartwood, from the centre of a tree, is in all respects dead, and samples from standing trees for carbon dating can usually be extracted by screwing in an 'increment borer' with a T-shaped handle. This technique relies on there being 'original' material in the tree to date, and is obviously not suitable for old baobabs that are hollow. Even solid baobabs are often so huge that extracting a sample of wood from the centre of a standing tree would need a borer far bigger and stronger than any produced thus far.

The increment borers in current use are far too small to extract complete samples from a large baobab.

The research of E R Swart was published in the May 18th 1963 issue of *Nature*. It focused on the results of carbon dating the wood of a baobab felled during the bush-clearing operations before the Zambezi River backed up behind Kariba Dam in Zimbabwe. With a radius of 2.28 m, wood samples were taken from its centre and from halfway between the centre and the outside. The centre sample was calculated to be 1 010 years old and that from midway 740 (each plus or minus 100 years). Leaving aside any inaccuracies of the technique, this is still one of the few scientific pieces of published research on a baobab's age.

In temperate climes, where years divide into definite seasons of growth and rest, counting annual rings is generally an accurate way of calculating tree ages. Rings show as concentric circles of light and dark wood, the large and light-coloured cells of spring and early summer growth contrasting with the darker, denser ones of autumn and winter. Nearer the equator temperatures may vary less, but baobab habitat is

Because most old baobabs are hollow, it is not possible to age them either by carbon dating original wood or by counting rings.

So, where does all this take us when it comes to discovering the age of *Adansonia digitata*? Often hollow, and with ill-defined rings, which may or may not be annual, it is a poor candidate for scientific dating. Even allowing for such rings as there are to be annual ones, the huge gnarled trunks of old baobabs are virtually impossible to saw through, and much too thick and twisted for complete samples to be extracted from their timber.

Michel Adanson made the first serious attempt to age baobabs. In 1749 he came across two on the Magdalene Islands off Cape Verde, one of which he estimated to be 5 150 years old. One hundred years later, Adanson's record found itself under attack by David Livingstone. His scientific bent was severely constrained by a dogmatic belief in the Creation theories of Bishop James Ussher, who had fixed the date of the world's creation at 23 October 4004 BC by counting the ages of Adam's descendants, as described in the Book of Genesis, and overlaying these on known dates of historic events.

The Archbishop went on to declare that the Ark touched down on Mount Ararat on 5 May 2348 BC. Anyone adhering rigidly to his timetable had to conclude that Adanson's

usually characterized by distinct rainy seasons, and rings certainly show on felled or fallen baobabs, especially once the trunk dries out and the wood starts to crack. (Actually, for baobabs, annual 'rings' is a misleading description, as more often one is trying to read parallel curved lines rather than concentric circles.) These rings probably indicate wet periods after dry. Whether they are annual or not depends on the seasonality of the climate. In parts of Africa with one distinct rainy season, rings may work out to be laid down yearly – droughts excepted. Baobabs growing furthest from the equator are most likely to show their ages in this way, particularly in southern Africa or Sudan where hot, usually wet, summers contrast with cold, rainless winters.

This hollow baobab was felled to make way for a rural electricity supply, and the rings in what is left of its wood are clearly visible. If there is only one rainy season where baobabs grow, such rings may be annual.

5 000-year-old trees would have been alive before the Great Flood. No tree could have survived the Great Flood. Adanson must have been wrong, or, even worse, was inferring the Flood was a fairy tale. In *Missionary Travels*, Livingstone, with a surprising touch of jingoism, writes that the baobab:

> *'... is the same as those which Adanson and others believed, from specimens seen in Western Africa, to have been alive before the flood. Arguing with a peculiar mental idiosyncracy resembling colour-blindness, common among the French of the time, these savans came to the conclusion that 'therefore there never was any flood'. I would back a true mowana [baobab] against a dozen floods, provided you do not boil it in hot sea-water; but I cannot believe that any of those now alive had a chance of being subjected to the experiment of even the Noachian deluge.'*

Ironically, perhaps, the oldest trees in the world are not growing in the lotus latitudes of the tropics. Continual warmth and frequent rain might seem to create an ideal environment for trees to live long lives, but in fact these conditions are generally better suited to fast growth; and growing fast and living long are, to some extent, mutually exclusive.

Only because elephants have been digging away at the trunk of this baobab in Tanzania's Tarangire National Park has its hollowness been revealed.

This tree fell naturally, but rings are still visible in its contorted wood.

It is not easy to determine the longest-lived species of tree, and there are a number of contenders. The line-up can be further confused by introducing trees that are growing out of truly ancient root stock, but are themselves of no great age. The dark, poisonous, red-berried yew (*Taxus baccata*) is one of these. Found all over Europe, east to the Himalayas and south into North Africa, some yews are almost certainly at least fuelled by rootstock well over 5 000 years old, even if the trees themselves are not this age.

The bristlecone pine (*Pinus longaeva*) is the other likely contender. The venerable specimen known as the Methuselah Tree has been carbon dated at 4 700 years old, and whole clumps of trees seem to be over 4 000. With half a year of night-time frosts and lots of snow, the pale, stony slopes of California's White Mountains provide an unlikely homeland for such ancient trees. Icy winds blast the mountains, rainfall is scant, and, like baobabs, the pines collect whatever water they can with a far-reaching network of near-surface roots.

As it dries out, decomposing baobab wood tends to separate into thick slices. Each of these represents the, often considerable, seasonal growth of a baobab.

Small does not necessarily mean young in the tree world; many of the baobabs growing in the harsh environment of Lekhubu Island could be just as old as the huge trees found elsewhere in Botswana.

In fine testimony to the diversity of California's landscape, further north, and closer to the sea, is the ancestral land of the ancient species of coast (*Sequoia sempervivens*) and giant redwoods (*Sequoiadendron giganteum*) known in Britain, where they grow very easily, as Wellingtonia, in tribute to the Duke. In California, high rainfall and summer mists create ideal conditions for these towering trees, which once grew all over the Pacific Northwest before their range began shrinking under the relentless assaults of axe and saw. Enough of these trees have been cut down for many sets of rings to have been counted, and 3 200 years seems about the oldest recorded.

Big baobabs are old, and most old specimens are big, but small trees are not necessarily young. Access to moisture is crucial to the size of a tree whose wood is three quarters water. The wizened baobabs on Botswana's Lekhubu Island seem to grow straight out of the rocks. Roots must find their way down between the cracks to such sandy soil as there is below, and most of whatever rain that falls drains off the slabs of stone, with little benefit to the trees. Yet these twisted and contorted baobabs may be just as old as the massive six-trunked bulk of Chapman's baobab. And even big trees seem to reach a stage in later life when expansion slows,

Measuring trees in the baobab plantation at Gedi on the Kenya coast. Despite being planted out at the same time, their growth rates differ dramatically.

before intake of food and water becomes just enough to maintain their existing dimensions and growth is suspended altogether.

There is much evidence to show that growth rates, and so eventually size, are genetically, as well as environmentally, determined. The painted plaque beside the grove of baobabs at Gedi Forest Nursery on the Kenyan coast informs visitors that the trees were planted in 1979. The grove appears to have begun with 49 seedlings, each set three yards from its neighbour, in a square seven trees by seven. There is very little sign of position favouring one tree over another, either then or now. At the end of November 2004, 39 remained of the original 49. Of these, 11 were over 100 cm around, measured at breast height, and seven were less than 60 cm. The largest baobab, 160 cm around

(179 cm in October 2006), was growing right next to the smallest, at 46 cm (49 cm in October 2006) – a huge difference, although probably accounted for in part, at least, by the larger tree drawing on the smaller one's resources.

There is nothing in the Gedi records to show the origins of the seeds from which these trees emerged. One can only assume that, if they did not all come from the same pod, they were at least representative samples of seeds from around the area. What this demonstrates is not so much the rate of baobab growth – those at Gedi are very close together, given their height and age, and are depriving each other of *lebensraum*. Rather, it shows how much genetic variation, whether in growth rates or any other characteristic, there is within a single population of trees.

When gazing at a huge and magnificent baobab, it is impossible to delink grandeur from age and to reach any other conclusion than that they must be among the most ancient trees in the world. What little scientific evidence there is to help age these trees at least supports the guesswork and conjecture, and baobabs can truly claim the title of the oldest trees in Africa, whether in terms of average age or the longevity of individual trees. They are also the fattest trees in Africa, a record rendered all the more extraordinary by the dryness of their surrounds.

Measuring a baobab

Baobab girth can be awkward to measure, the easiest method being to put a tape around the trunk. This works well during the tree's first few years, when baobab boles are roughly circular. Yet these trees live unpredictable existences, trunks twist and bend, developing indents and depressions, and big branches shoot off from close to the ground, all making circumference measurements increasingly irregular and subjective.

With oaks or beeches being the largest trees early European travellers had ever encountered, their first reaction on seeing an African baobab was often to estimate its girth. Measuring tapes were clearly not on most expeditions' equipment lists, leading explorers to employ confusingly disparate techniques to record a tree's dimensions. Cadamosto walked a tree 'seventeen paces round the foot' while Adanson was more scientific and:

'. . . extended my arms, as wide as possible I could, thirteen times, before I embraced its circumference; and for greater exactness, I measured it afterwards round with packthread, and found it to be sixty-five feet.'

A self-portrait of Thomas Baines sketching in April 1862 from the branches of a baobab tree near Lake Ngami in Botswana.
(With permission Royal Geographical Society, London)

The massive bulk of Chapman's baobab in Botswana beckons to travellers from far away. It was both camped under and measured by Chapman, Baines, Livingstone, and many others.

Thomas Baines explored a lot of Namibia and northern Botswana, but does not appear to have accurately taped any of the trees he described or painted. On 22 July 1858, while on the fateful journey when Livingstone would accuse him of stealing stores, he 'measured' a baobab:

'. . . equal in circumference to twelve times the length of my extended arms, which estimating my fathom at only five feet would give a measurement of sixty'.

Later, on the Northern Goldfields Expedition of 1871, he found a baobab, '10 times the span of my extended arms or, perhaps, nearly 50 feet'. From this we can at least discern that Baines's reach had not diminished in 13 years.

The tree that so astounded James Chapman in 1852 had a 'circumference at the base to be twenty-nine yards'. A year later Livingstone found himself camped under the same tree 'of six branches united into one trunk. At three feet off the ground it was eighty-five feet in circumference', only two feet less than Chapman's measurement. The difference could, at least in part, be accounted for by Chapman's having been taken at ground level, or simply by dry season contraction.

Charles Sweeney describes his time in the Nuba Mountains of southern Sudan in *Background of Baobabs*. There, the average girth of 845 trees, taken about a metre off the ground, measured 7.5 m. From these and a mass of other reported measurements, it would be safe to say that 15 m is a big tree, over 20 m exceptional, and anything more than 25 worthy of entry in the record books. West African trees seem to be smaller, and the largest reported from Senegal in *Notes Africaines* was 21 m. Swart's carbon dated, 1 000-year-old tree was 14 m around its trunk.

Scientifically, girth is sometimes measured at ground level (GGL), occasionally at waist height (GWH), and most often at breast height (GBH), which now seems to have standardized at 1.3 m. Measurements are taken by stretching a cord around the trunk. This produces some distorted results, particularly on concave trunks or those with protruding ridges; however, the technique is clear and easily executed, and different people measuring the same tree are likely to come up with roughly similar figures. This is more than can be said of the alternative which has the tape contouring the trunk to take account of cracks and indentations – the *méthode des sinuosites*, as *Notes Africaines* put it, against the *méthode de la corde tendue*. Figures arrived at in this way can be very subjective, as one person may take account of a particularly deep fissure in the trunk that another may ignore.

Even given a standardized measuring method, comparing the girth of the same tree at different times in its life can be misleading. Measured again in 1966, Chapman's tree was down to 80 ft in circumference. This and other similar comparisons are used to support arguments either that baobabs, particularly hollow ones, shrink with age, or that they expand and contract in wet and dry weather. Both may be true, but had elephants, perhaps, dug away at the trunk some time during the previous 100 years, or could local people have harvested successive rings of bark for rope- or basket-making? Was erosion around the bottom of the tree enough to give recent height above the ground a noticeably lower base point? Much of the root system under the canopy of Chapman's tree has been exposed, the ground gradually worn away by the shuffling feet of generations of itinerant Bushmen, Tswana settlers, Chapman, Livingstone, and motor-borne visitors like me.

From some angles it seems as if the fused trunks of Namibia's Grootboom could consist of more than one tree.

Baobabs are best documented in southern Africa, with its far-reaching network of roads and long-established scientific societies. In 1982, South Africa's Dendrological Foundation established a National Register of Big Trees. After three years of record collecting, only one baobab topped the 25 m girth; this specimen was a massive 33 m (although a metre shorter than two trees of 14 and 19 m around).

Near Duiwelskloof in South Africa is a baobab which the owners of the land on which it grows describe in their publicity material as the biggest in the world. Claiming a circumference of 46.8 m, their contention may well be justified, with or without entry in the Dendrological Foundation's register. The tree comprises two vast and distinct trunks, similar in size and fused together at the bottom. As well as complicating the measuring process, this raises the question whether the trunks emerged from different seeds or not.

It may seem more natural for the biggest baobabs to be growing in the heart of their range, not right down at their southernmost limits. However, in northern Botswana and northeast Namibia there are vast trees, magnificent both in girth and height. With the *méthode de la corde tendue* I measured the Grootboom, near Tsumkwe, at 29.5 m. Using the *méthode des sinuosites* to take account of larger indents it came out at 32.6 m around. Even more stupendous was its height – well over 30 m, and if ever there is a search for the baobab of greatest volume, this is my nominee.

When all the science is said and the measuring done, knowing when a baobab first pushed its

The Green brothers were Canadian hunters based in South Africa, and evidence of their passing is clearly legible in the eponymous tree – 'GREEN'S EXPEDITION 1858,9'.

bright green shoot above the surface of the Earth is the only really accurate way to age it. The chains of human memory, which should link the past with the present, are disconcertingly fragile and, in the end, unreliable. In the African countryside trees may be remembered as having appeared the same year as the firstborn son of a chief, and sometimes even planted to celebrate a special occasion. The emergence of other trees may be connected to the rainstorm that relieved the worst of all droughts – events yes, but seldom dates.

Written or photographic history is relatively new to Africa and is of little help in ageing things as ancient as baobab trees. The oldest written descriptions of a quintessentially African tree are actually of a specimen outside the continent. Allahabad, known in its pre-Islamic life as Pratishthana, has always been a holy city, marked on ancient maps as the place where the Yamuna River joins the Ganges. Chinese explorer Hiuen Tsang visited this sacred confluence about 630 AD and wrote of a 'celebrated Deva Temple in front of which was a great wide-spreading umbrageous tree'. In 1575, when Moghul emperor Akhbar the Great entered the town, he found 'infidels . . . with a desire to obtain the rewards that are promised in their creed . . . casting themselves down into the deep river from the top of a high tree'. This tree has an average diameter of over 6 m and a vast mound of a trunk from which several thick branches sprout. From a distance it looks like a banyan tree (*Ficus benghalensis*), but it is in fact a baobab.

While the tradition of written African history is short-lived, there is a wealth of painted African art on cave walls and cliff overhangs. Surprisingly little depicts trees and plants. Baobabs have been vital in sustaining Africa's primates, right through to *Homo*'s emergence as *sapiens* and beyond. If early African art was simply the product of representational skill and imagination, it seems inconceivable that the artists would not have included these trees in their paintings. Many authorities opine that much of this art represents experiences in trance-like states of altered consciousness. If the supernatural powers channelled through these artists derived from animals – particularly eland, kudu, sable and giraffe – this may go some way to explain the paucity of painted trees.

If human depictions of baobabs on cave walls are inexplicably scarce, mankind has left many signs of his passing on the actual tree, sometimes etched deep enough in its trunk to last the rest of its life. Two hundred and fifty years ago European governments encouraged sailors arriving in strange anchorages to leave evidence of their arrival before the ships of rival colonial powers. Overland explorers were similarly keen to record their passing, and Livingstone is said to have etched 'DL' into the bark of both Chapman's baobab and a tree near Victoria Falls, as well as inside a hollow baobab near the mouth of the Zambezi River.

Further west, and ten years after Livingstone's death, Dorsland trekkers began their exodus from South Africa, escaping British colonial dominance and threats to their freedom of worship. The scattering of their historical and religious monuments shows clearly the different routes they took on the great trek up to Angola.

One hundred and twenty years of history are etched into the bark of the Dorsland Tree in Namibia.

One of these groups passed a huge baobab, now known as the Dorsland Tree, on which they carved '1883'. Not long after, realizing the only way to secure Namibia was to run it as a true colony, Germany dispatched Schutztruppe to enforce its occupation. A detachment of these troops went past the Dorsland Tree too, and at least three of them, H Gathemann, E Heller and D Hannemann, engraved their names and '1891'.

I passed by to pay my respects to the Dorsland Tree, not by ox wagon or on the back of a horse, but on four wheels. It was 112 years since the Schutztruppe's visit, and I felt an easy sense of contact with them in seeing the work of their hands exactly where they had made it. The tree was bare, backed by a watery evening sun, setting behind the cracked mud of a waterhole. Skinks scurried in and out of holes in its trunk, and a swallow-tailed bee-eater darted from a perch at passing insects. The few fruit that hung rather sadly from its branches seemed to imply that this giant of a tree was using most of its dwindling energies merely staying alive, and soon even doing this would take more than it had left.

Evidence that a huge tree was huge 100 or 200 years ago offers no help in ageing it, only in placing it in the context of human history. Recent writings, while verifying the ages of many young baobabs, make no contribution to the debate on how old is really old. No ancient African trees are set down in written records to speak their ages for the species. So, perhaps thankfully, the conjecture continues, and taxi drivers from Dhaka to Dar es Salaam, Angola to Ethiopia, can continue pointing out the oldest baobab in the world. And who can prove them wrong?

In the words of W H Auden, 'knowledge may have its purpose, but guessing is always more fun than knowing'.

Elephants pose a threat to the longevity of baobabs, however healthy and resilient these trees may seem.

CHAPTER SIX
A forest in itself

'In short the whole of this calabash tree seemed to form a forest in itself' was Michel Adanson's conclusion on first describing a baobab tree. Wherever they grow, baobabs nurture their own micro-communities of plants and animals. Some animals are casual visitors to baobabs, using them simply because they are big trees – usually the biggest ones around, and so offer the highest vantage points, the best hunting ground or the largest choice of nest sites. Other animals make use of traits, such as hollowness or wrinkled bark, which these trees provide much more generously than any others do.

PREVIOUS PAGES: Red-billed buffalo weavers have built their untidy nests in this baobab in the Kruger National Park in South Africa.
OPPOSITE: Baobabs stretching up the hillside from the Great Ruaha River in central Tanzania.
ABOVE AND OVERLEAF: Both baobabs and desert roses store water in their trunks, and both are often in flower when nothing else is.

A Tanzanian community

In southern Tanzania, on the way from Morogoro to Iringa, the road winds down into the valley of the Great Ruaha River. The very name resonates with all that is most wild, mysterious and romantic about Africa, and the river does not disappoint. The road follows its northern bank for about 20 km as it cuts through the northern end of the Udzungwa Mountains, creating what is locally known as Baobab Valley.

The trees stretch away from the river, grey, sometimes pinky, trunks reflecting back the sunlight far up the slopes. Those growing on flatter ground, closer to the road, are larger, and so appear older than the smaller more distant ones. In fact, baobabs on more level land will always grow much bigger, both food and water being more plentiful and easily absorbed than if they were clinging to a stony hillside.

This was July, that time of year when life in Africa seems to be marking time, awaiting the press of some hidden hormonal trigger to restart it. For once nearly all the baobabs seemed to be marching to the beat of the same biological drum, bare, scarcely a leaf, flower or fruit to be seen.

The baobabs dominated the valley's vegetation, yet they were only one part of a mosaic of trees and shrubs that covered this dried land. A tangled mass of impenetrable acacia and *Commiphora* bush, mostly bare-branched, grew like a barbed wire fence along the roadside. A few *Acacia mellifera* displayed their creamy white blooms on bare branches, and all over the hillsides, in among the baobabs, bright clumps of pink desert roses stood out against the rocks and desiccated vegetation.

Even in late morning sunbirds were flitting among the baobabs, although they seemed to be using these as mere staging posts on their way

Leopard orchids (*Ansellia africana*) are distributed from sea level to well above the altitudinal limit for baobabs, and clumps of this epiphyte are sometimes seen festooning the silhouettes of these trees.

to the acacia blossoms. Brown parrots flashed their green rumps in flight, and ashy starlings were visible among the bare branches or pecking around on the ground below. Crowned and Von der Decken's hornbills swooped between the trees with typically undulating flight.

Baboons were playing their daredevil games along the roadside. Were they so prolific because there was so much baobab fruit to feast on every year? Or were there so many baobabs because the baboons were doing such a good job dispersing seeds? The answer was probably yes to both questions. There were also very few people around to persecute the monkeys and not a lot of livestock to nibble off the tips of young baobabs. The inhabitants of the few small roadside settlements had preserved the baobabs around their huts,

although some had that lopped look, suggesting branches were being cut so domestic animals could eat young leaves.

On the far side of the river is the protected part of the Udzungwa Mountains. There, four greater kudu picked their way down between the baobabs to the river, a male with magnificent spiralling horns, a smaller male and two lighter-coloured females. Baboons were drinking just upstream of the kudu, and downstream a crocodile feigned sleep on a sandbank.

Here was a community of which baobabs were a component, crucial to the existence of some of the other plants and animals, less important to others. Many of the different plants, which together create a community, simply share the same space. They require similar conditions, and are as likely to compete for light, water, food and space as to benefit from each other's presence. Some species may offer incidental shade, shelter or support to others, and the decaying leaves of one may nourish young plants of another. Yet, occasionally, a tree of a different species grows so close to a baobab, and looks so healthy, it seems at least one of them is actively benefiting in some way from this closeness. Black thorn acacia (*Acacia mellifera*), desert date (*Balanites aegyptiaca*) or tamarind (*Tamarindus indica*), often flourish in the shelter of big baobabs, almost trunk to trunk, sharing resources seemingly to the detriment of neither.

Some inter-plant relationships are more intimate. Epiphytes, like lichens and mosses, depend on their host for nothing more than a

Although orchids typically prefer cool, damp climates, this one (*Angraecum* sp.) is growing on the trunk of a baobab at Gedi on the Kenya coast.

secure place to grow. Nestling snugly on the bark or in a cleft between a tree's branches, epiphytes gather sustenance from the atmosphere or from decomposing plant matter that collects around their roots. Being so smooth-barked, the flat upper surfaces of baobab branches seldom offer epiphytes good rootholds, but the cracks, folds and forks in the tree make ideal sheltered refuges where seeds germinate easily and growth can continue undisturbed. Many orchids are epiphytic, growing in clumps on big branches or in clefts between the limbs of a tree. As a whole, African members of the Orchidaceae family prefer cool, damp environments, but a few species are suited to the warmth of baobab territory.

Passive lodgers though epiphytes may be, some cause the death of their host as certainly as any parasite would. A violet-backed starling or orange-bellied parrot flies away from a fruiting fig tree and deposits its seed-laden droppings in the fork of a nearby baobab. This simple act may sentence the baobab to death as effectively as the first cut of an axe – although it may be a hundred years before the tree finally sheds its last leaf.

Figs

Ficus is a large genus, whose best-known species are probably the multiple-trunked banyan tree and the sacred bodhi fig (*Ficus religiosa*), both endemic to the Asian subcontinent. It is also strongly represented in Africa, where many of the species are epiphytic. 'Strangler fig' describes those figs starting life in the fork of a mature tree (as does the banyan), which they eventually kill. Once seeds have germinated, and the seedlings are well settled on their host, the stranglers send down aerial roots. These claw their way to the ground where they take hold and begin channelling water and minerals to the leaves and branches. What was a root slowly starts to function as a trunk.

Looking at a baobab in the embrace of the thick, snaking trunk-roots of a fig, it is often difficult to separate the strangler from the strangled. The outside of the wooden bole seems to be all fig, but inside, some of the baobab's trunk may still provide a conduit to channel nourishment to its branches. Often, the only way to gauge if the baobab is still a living, functioning organism is by examining the leaf canopy. When both fig and baobab are in leaf, fig leaves look an even darker green. Although most African figs are deciduous, they may still be in leaf when baobabs are not; then the baobab branches protrude nakedly from the clusters of fig leaves, as if clutching vainly at the air for help.

LEFT AND ABOVE: The trunk of a 'strangler fig' acts like a straitjacket, preventing the baobab from growing and eventually depriving it of enough food and water to remain alive.

Despite their name, strangler figs do not actually squeeze the life out of their host. The fig acts more like a straitjacket, enveloping the baobab trunk and preventing the host from growing. Slowly the fig begins to dominate the competition for water and light. The baobab trunk, no longer able to form any new sapwood, ages into heartwood and, after absorbing its own goodness, begins rotting. Finally, the fig emerges as a perfect tree on its own.

Rain running down the branches deposits dust, dead leaves and nutrients in the fork of a baobab trunk. These micro-catchments stay damp much longer than the surrounding soil. As well as nourishing orchids and other epiphytes, they can prove such fertile growing grounds that almost any seed brought there by birds, small animals, wind or water stands a fair chance of germinating.

Apart from strangler figs, none of these accidental arrivals will cause the baobab much more direct harm than to add weight to already burdened branches. Of far more obvious danger are parasitic plants, which extract moisture and nourishment from their hosts. Some parasites, like mistletoe, have well-developed leaves with plenty of chlorophyll, and so can produce much of their own nourishment. Others have lesser or even no leaves and are more dependent on sustenance from the plants on which they are fixed.

OPPOSITE TOP: The dark green fig protrudes above the baobab, which should survive many more years before it is finally killed by its host.
OPPOSITE BOTTOM: This fig now completely dominates the baobab, whose few bare branches show among the foliage of the epiphyte.
LEFT: The baobab has completely disintegrated, leaving only the surrounding fig trunk, which will eventually fill the void left by its host.
BELOW: Hundreds of years ago, this perfectly shaped fig tree probably began life in the fork of a baobab branch.

ABOVE: Elephants chew species of the genus *Sansevieria* to extract moisture from the fibrous leaves. It is unusual to find a clump of such greenery in the fork of a baobab tree.
LEFT: Prickly pear (*Opuntia vulgaris*) growing in the cleft of a branch of an Eritrean baobab, the seed probably dropped there by a bird.
OPPOSITE: The taxonomy of African mushrooms has a long way to go; these ones, growing inside a fallen baobab trunk, may belong to the genus *Volvariella*; they tasted like the baobab god's ambrosia.

The soil beneath deciduous trees is enriched by the humus of decomposing leaves. Both plants and fungi are attracted to this ideal growing ground, and some species have a particular affinity for the moist shade beneath baobab trees. African mushrooms usually have no English names, and the knowledge of their edibility and other ethnobotanical information often rests in the memories of a few tribal elders. Along the Kenya coast, the Giriama identify pink-gilled, slender-stalked mushrooms, growing only in the hollow trunks of fallen baobabs, as *Zhoga muyu* – 'mushroom of the baobab'.

As well as the passive plant and fungal life living on or around baobabs, an array of birds and animals relies on the trees for necessities of life. Many of these smaller creatures spend their whole lives in the same tree, contributing to the composition of each baobab's own miniature ecosystem. Others visit for food, shelter, rest or to raise their young. James Chapman, in *Travels in the Interior of South Africa* (1868), was struck by the baobab's great community:

'These trees are the resort of innumerable squirrels, mice, lizards, snakes, and also a small winged insect, called palele. When these insects alight on the human frame, they generally deposit a fluid, which soon induces a painful irritation and small white blisters. It seems to be a kind of vine-bug. Very fine hives, with honey, are often found in the baobab, and many of the larger birds delight to build their nests in them.'

In his Appendix, Chapman details not only the uses to which local people put various parts of the tree, but also the shade and shelter it may give to 'troops of gnus, buffaloes and the mighty elephant himself'.

Surviving elephants

Baobabs are the biggest living things in their environments. Elephants are the largest land mammals on earth, and the longest-lived. They once wandered all over sub-Saharan Africa. Almost everywhere a baobab grew there were elephants, and the destinies of the two have been inextricably linked throughout their mutual evolution.

Today, although the extent of their coexistence is drastically reduced, baobabs and elephants still survive together. Elephants extract much goodness from baobabs, often at great cost to the trees, which are damaged to an extent that would easily kill any other species. To have survived so long in the African savanna, and yet continued appealing to elephants, baobabs needed unique resilience and powers of recovery. These they have, and elephant damage is seldom fatal.

Elephants occasionally chew baobab twigs, but without any real enthusiasm for them; they prefer to dig away at the trunks.

Baobab bark is exceptionally rich in calcium, one of the reasons why elephants are so attracted to it. They first dig into the tree with their tusks, tearing the bark into strips and then ripping these off with their trunks. Then they may start on the wood, which is soft and moist, chewing it to extract nourishment, then spitting out the stringy fibre.

Baobabs all over the plains and hillsides of Tanzania's Tarangire National Park show the full spectrum of elephant damage. Scarcely a tree has gone untouched. Least affected are those whose bark was stripped off years ago, leaving scars far up the trunk as the only evidence of elephants' attentions. Others have been lacerated more recently, and hanging off their trunks are tattered strips of grey and chestnut fibre, in contrast to the lighter shreds of inner wood. Where elephants have lingered longer, great wedges have been gouged out of the trees.

The damage baobabs can seemingly sustain, while giving every indication of remaining in good health, means revising some of the preconceived notions about what will kill a tree. The baobab's powers of survival are vastly superior to those of almost any other species. Some baobabs live with no more than half their trunk intact, appearing to defy the laws of both nature and gravity. As long as a baobab remains standing it seems to stay alive.

Elephants can work their way round younger baobabs until these are supported by no more than a thin central cylinder of wood, like the waist of an hourglass. Even if the tree does not fall over, a lot of moisture may be lost from its exposed trunk, leaving it more vulnerable to drought or disease. For older, hollow baobabs the mechanics of support and collapse are different. Having lost their heartwood centres, hollow trees depend for support on outer sapwood walls. If elephants gouge out too much from one side or the other, those trees will inevitably topple over.

If baobabs responded to damage as most trees do, they could never have endured so long in the face of elephant appetites. They needed to evolve an ability to withstand abnormally severe damage, and they have. If they had not, to survive would have meant gradually developing other defences against elephants, like ferocious thorns, a foul taste, much harder wood or poisonous sap. Yet for all the baobab's resilience, when truly stressed, elephants can damage whole populations of trees so badly these may look as if they will never recover. During a terrible drought in the early 1960s, elephants in Kenya's Tsavo National Park began to target baobabs so determinedly that they completely altered the park's landscape. Today, the baobab population still looks healthier outside the park than in.

Even in that Utopian age when elephants moved around Africa wherever they wished, rather than wherever they could, populations of baobabs and elephants are likely to have continually fluctuated. The cycle of rain

Damage like this would kill any other species of tree, but this baobab showed a fine canopy of leaves.

Almost in an act of final retribution, this baobab in Tarangire National Park crushed the elephant that toppled it.

Elephants often target younger, more succulent, baobabs.

after drought after rain has sustained life in Africa since long before man stood up. In wet times many baobab seeds germinated and, with plenty of alternative food, the elephants allowed the trees to flourish. Then came dry years, which would be bad for both elephants and baobabs. Do these short-term imbalances not actually amount to long-term stability? And is the spur to evolutionary change not instability rather than equilibrium anyway?

In the context of their long lives, the elephants' range has contracted frighteningly fast, in two or three generations, which is less than a single generation for baobabs. Just how fast is never better evidenced than by the elephant-scarred trunks of thousands of baobabs on what are now newly settled small-scale farms around the edges of national parks.

Living in harmony

Other creatures nourish themselves in decidedly less dramatic, and less damaging, ways on different parts of the tree. Flowers, fruit and leaves all provide sustenance for animals and birds with less hardened digestive systems than the elephant's. For some animals, at least one of these by-products of the baobab's annual cycle may be an important component of their diet; other animals may be merely tempted by morsels of flower or leaf in times of near-starvation.

Nectar is the pollinator's prime reward for visiting baobab flowers, but other creatures extract this thick sugary juice without contributing to the next generation of trees. Sunbirds manage to perch on the sepals and lean over to stick their beaks – perfectly curved for the operation –

The baobab's fallen flowers seem to be one of nature's least utilized by-products, instantly redundant once they hit the ground, and ignored by most creatures as a source of food.

between the bases of petals, extracting nectar without going anywhere near the pollen-tipped stamens. Male scarlet-chested sunbirds look particularly magnificent in their search for sugar, their spectacular red chests, green heads and browny-black bodies in stark contrast to the creamy white flowers and brilliant blue of the sky. Green wood-hoopoes are shiny-black, long-tailed birds with elegantly curved red beaks. They travel in noisy parties, always rushing to move on to the next tree. However, for a feast of baobab nectar they seem perfectly prepared to risk losing their companions, perching on nearby twigs and easily hooking their beaks between the sepals and petals of any flowers within reach.

With the countryside often so parched and barren when baobabs start blooming, their flowers may constitute food of last resort. In October 2000, after six dry months, a few baobabs in Kenya's Meru National Park were showing early white blooms. One of these had been invaded by a troop of vervet monkeys, which seemed desperate to get at the flowers. These they first snapped off at the stalk before hurriedly pulling at the petals, which they dropped, together with the stamens, onto the ground. All that remained was stalk, sepals and the undeveloped ovary, and something there seemed to offer them a worthwhile bite. However, sifting through the discards below the tree after the monkeys had left, I found the sepals and ovary still intact. Only later did I find out what had probably attracted the monkeys: the globs of nectar they could lick from the underside of the sepals, after pulling off the rest of the flower. I have since heard of colobus monkeys behaving in the same way at the Kenya coast.

By daybreak, baobab flowers start to wilt, and when the corolla plops onto the ground, ants start searching for the sugary nectar. The petals wilt and darken, and the remains slowly crumble into dust. Tannin in the petals causes them to brown very quickly, and also makes them bitter tasting. There are very few written references to mammals – usually impala or eland – nibbling at freshly fallen flowers.

In this case though, the record tells only part of the story. Munyao Mwakavi is a Wakamba driver, old enough to have some grey hairs and also to remember a much wilder environment than exists today. As a youth he would build a platform in a tree next to a flowering baobab, and wait with his bow and arrow for bushbuck to emerge in the evening from their daytime cover and start grazing on fallen flowers. Sometimes Munyao would even scatter handfuls of flowers below his perch, to give himself a better chance of shooting the animals cleanly. Now the bushbuck have gone, to be replaced by goats and sheep, and as soon as he lets these out every morning, they too scamper over to the nearest baobab to see if any flowers fell in the night.

Hungry animals are more attracted to the tender, pale green leaf shoots, which may also start appearing while the landscape awaits the first rains. If elephants are around, they will graze most of the twigs and greenery off the lower branches, leaving nothing for any land-bound creature shorter than a giraffe. The best chance other herbivores get to feed on baobab leaves is offered by any newly fallen trees with roots still well enough connected to channel water to the branches.

Cracks and hollows

Hollow baobab trunks make ideal bat roosts for many species of bizarre-sounding insectivorous bats, such as free-tailed, leaf-nosed, flat-headed and wrinkle-lipped. Fruit bats, particularly the Egyptian fruit bat, upon whose appetite the future of *Adansonia digitata* largely depends, usually roost

Its small eyes immediately identify this bat inside a hollow baobab as an echo-locating insectivore, perhaps one of the many species of free-tailed bats (Molossidae).

Harmless millipedes (Diplopoda) are particularly active at night and in the rainy season; they may find refuge in baobab trunks, but feed among leaf litter on the ground.

in thousands in caves. Quickly exhausting the local food supplies, they must often travel great distances to find fruit or flowers.

Late one afternoon I had squeezed into a hollow baobab in Tanzania, before my torch revealed the inside walls lined with twittering bats. Unsettled by the light, they began fluttering around, sensing they might be safer outside than in. The thought of these bats streaming past my face, out of a hole I was partly blocking, was enough to send me into reverse, until I noticed another chink of light further up the trunk. This was surely their exit and, with the torch off, calm soon returned. Easing my way out, I waited until dusk to watch the bats leave their roost. As they spilled out of their baobab refuge, black against the grey sky over the grey sea,

there seemed a satisfying symmetry in the thought that some of them might find baobab flowers to pollinate that night.

Cracks and wrinkles in the baobab bark, forks between branches, splintery stubs of broken limbs, rotting holes in the trunk – all provide wonderful shelters for insects and other small creatures. Geckos scuttle up and down the trunk in search of insects, flattening themselves against the bark. Out on the branch tips, weaving webs between the twig ends, are all sorts of spiders, including the buffalo spider, an arachnophobe's nightmare with big 'antlers', and black and red stripes on a bright yellow body.

One of the attractions of the baobab as a refuge, especially after many rainless months, is the water left in hollow trunks or the moisture that remains in the soil around the roots. Reptiles need to drink, and arboreal snakes like the black mamba, boomslang and twig snakes may use baobabs as a resting place until the rains come. Spitting or Egyptian cobras seek shelter in tree holes closer to the ground, and burrowing species of skinks will look for damp earth. Some agamas and other lizards are permanent members of a baobab's community; others move from tree to tree as the seasons prescribe.

Chameleons, which are also lizards, walk ponderously along shiny baobab branches, searching for insects to scoop up with their long, unfurling tongues. Green praying mantises live among the foliage, nabbing caterpillars off the leaves – that is if the females are not sated from devouring their mates. For most mantises safety depends on being able to pose as twigs. Stick insects resemble mantises, although the two are not closely related. They stalk around baobab branches, often at least one leg short of their full insect quota of six, in search of choice mouthfuls of vegetation, while avoiding the attentions of ants, birds and lizards.

Birds and bees

Honeybees also lodge in baobab trees, taking advantage of clefts in the trunk or holes in branches to make their nests. Most of their food comes from other plants once these start flowering, although some bees may visit the flowers of their home tree in the early morning before the blooms fall to the ground. Looking out for bees' nests on approaching a baobab is a

The pegs of a honey hunter's ladder are a sure sign that bees once nested in the tree, and may still do so.

wise precaution. Blundering up to a tree only to find bees buzzing in and out of a hole at eye level makes for a nervous retreat.

Bees' nests can be difficult to spot, particularly in dry weather when their inhabitants are generally inactive. The waxy combs may be visible as they are darker than the baobab bark on the edge of the nest hole. The hardwood sticks of human honey hunters' ladders, or footholds cut into the trunk, lead unerringly to nest sites, although these are often deserted, and the only climbers may be baboons searching for fruit.

There is no more intriguing way to find a bees' nest than to be shown it by a greater honeyguide. At the southern end of the rocky backbone of Tarangire National Park is a huge hollow baobab, known, like many others elsewhere in Africa, as the Poacher's Hideout. In April one year it was in full, luxuriant leaf, as was another nearby tree that offered shade for a midday picnic. Up above, a smallish, insignificantly plumaged bird began to fuss and flutter and, as soon as I reached for my binoculars, it flew down onto the top of a thorn bush. I made out distinctive pale cheeks, but was still struggling with identification when it took off again, this time into the Poacher's Hideout. Convinced I had lost the bird among the foliage, I looked up and saw it fluttering away as if desperate I should keep it in sight. Then everything fell into place. Right next to the branch where it was displaying was a huge bees' nest, which the bird was showing me – playing the perfect role described for it by the scientific name *Indicator indicator*.

Many other birds perch, roost, nest and feed in baobabs. Most use the trees for no other reason than that they are the tallest and most hollow trees around. Parrots and their diminutives, lovebirds, have a close affinity for baobabs. Wherever their ranges overlap the birds seem greatly attracted to the trees. They often nest in holes in the trunk,

Baobab holes provide favoured nesting sites for yellow-billed hornbills; this male will feed his mate while she is walled inside her nest.

This marabou stork is using the top of a baobab tree as no more than a lookout station.

waddling clumsily around the branches, in distinct contrast to the screeching agility they show in the air. Yellow-bellied parrots are said to eat baobab seeds, but otherwise the trees provide very little of the shoots, fruit and small seeds that make up the diets of all species of *Poicephalus*.

Bigger baobab holes make good nest sites for several hornbills of the genus *Tockus*, particularly red-billed, yellow-billed, Von der Decken's and African grey. The females go to the dramatic lengths of sealing themselves into the holes with mud and droppings for the duration of incubation, as well as the first few weeks after the young have tapped their way out of their eggshells. During confinement the females lose all their feathers, while the monogamous males push fruit, insects and other small animals through the cracks left open in the earthen wall. Two or three weeks after the chicks have hatched, the female pecks open a hole large enough to squeeze through and leaves the nest. The chicks reseal the hole, using their own droppings, leaving a slit through which both parents can now feed them. Seven weeks after hatching, the chicks finally exchange their keyhole view of the outside world for a panoramic sweep of African savanna.

Owls, barbets, woodpeckers and rollers roost or nest in baobab holes too. Owls also roost out in the open, often edging close up to the trunk in the hope of being less conspicuous and harder for small birds to mob. Rollers use the branches as lookout perches. I once watched a pair of lilac-breasted rollers courting each other outside a small hole in the trunk of a Tanzanian sea-edge baobab. The male fluttered excitedly around his mate, then they both launched into great sweeping

Black-headed (village) weavers often occupy the same tree for years on end, and from a distance their nests look like the fruit on a baobab.

circles of flight before the male landed back on the lip of the hole and disappeared inside. The female waited quietly on the branch outside before the male emerged, and in that clumsy-seeming, yet extraordinarily elegant way of birds, fluttered on top of her and mated.

Perching is a serious business for rollers, which seem permanently on the watch for other birds entering their territories, as well as for food. Many raptors also use the tops of leafless baobabs as vantage points, especially those that hunt from perches. Brown snake eagles are especially associated with baobabs, often in cultivated areas where the trees have been spared. They, too, move from perch to perch, but need to spend much longer on each, searching for the slow slither of a hunting snake, or for movements of the cryptically camouflaged puff adder, which is favoured prey despite its size and toxicity. Wahlberg's eagle also watches over cleared ground between big trees. This small, almost kite-like predator regularly nests in baobabs. It never hunts birds near its home tree, and so weavers, starlings and other tree dwellers are attracted to nest there by the protection from snakes that the eagle offers.

Away from the trunk, other birds may be nesting, and down towards the end of the branches, where they are better protected from egg or nestling predators, weavers build their distinctive nests. Baobabs particularly suit those species that make nests of dry grass or twigs. Red-headed weavers construct untidy looking nests with long entrance tubes; they are not communal nesters and if several nests are hanging off the end of the same slender branch it is usually because each year they build a new nest next to last season's. Near human habitation baobabs are occasionally taken over by noisy breeding colonies of black-headed (or village) weavers, seeking their protection from predators by proximity to mankind.

Hamerkops may build their enormous domed nests in any suitable cleft in a tree, often near water; once abandoned, nests may be taken over by Egyptian geese.

The most conspicuous nests are the untidy communal structures built by red-billed buffalo weavers, which, from a distance, make baobabs seem afflicted by some parasitic growth. In true weaver fashion only males build the nests, often over several months, then show them to the females. The weavers fortify their nests with acacia twigs as a further deterrent to invading snakes, such as the tree-living boomslang. The snake slithers around the ends of baobab branches during the daytime, particularly if there are young in the nests. The following season, abandoned buffalo weaver nests may be taken over by superb starlings, which have higher comfort requirements than the former owners and line the nests with grass.

In some places, buffalo weavers are believed to nest only on the western side of a baobab, and so to serve as a compass for disoriented travellers. In Namibia I looked at hundreds of buffalo weaver nests. There, the birds seemed definitely to favour

the northern side of the trees, perhaps so the young could get as much sun as possible. More likely though, weavers site their nests on the leeward side of a tree, where they are best protected from the wind. This would still allow nests to serve as direction finders, but only with the knowledge of the quarter from which the wind usually blows.

Take away the baobabs, and a whole community disappears with them. Shade, shelter, food, breeding places, hunting lookouts; the loss of a baobab is much more than the loss of a tree.

Still shattered by the after-effects of World War II, with the prospects of food rationing stretching on interminably, Britain's government conceived a massive scheme to alleviate the world's shortage of edible fats and oils: to cover more than three million acres of Tanganyika with peanuts. When lack of rain compounded the disasters afflicting the 'Ground Nut Scheme', attempts were made to salvage something from its wreckage by planting sunflowers instead of peanuts. Early indications were that this might be successful, and in a letter to *The Times*, a Dr Harland calculated that to fill 24 000 acres would take 34 million sunflowers. Then another correspondent asked whether there were enough bees to pollinate all these sunflowers. As far as could be seen, there were almost no bees at all. Why were there no bees? Because after clearing the bush no baobabs were left for them to nest in.

From a distance, clumps of leopard orchids look like the nests of red-billed buffalo weavers.

CHAPTER SEVEN

A hermit in its shade

The baobab tree is some things to many people, and many things to some. It is food for humans and their animals, a pharmacy to treat tropical sickness, and a provider of raw materials for almost limitless uses. In the April 1962 issue of *Notes Africaines* from Senegal, J G Adam concludes that 'in reading of the variety of uses for the different parts of the baobab, a wise man would almost be tempted to take up the life of a hermit in its shade; he will lack for nothing in his life if he chooses his subject well'.

PREVIOUS PAGES: Bark is usually harvested from the trunk, but, for bow strings, this Hadzabe hunter in Tanzania preferred to strip it from young branches at the top of the tree.
ABOVE: Despite such drastic ringbarking, this Malian tree will heal completely and, as little as six years later, the process can be repeated.

Bark and fibre

The very essence of the baobab is contained in its trunk. The same regenerative powers that enable baobabs to survive excavations by elephants also allow bark to be harvested many times in the tree's life. The idea that a tree can easily survive repeated ringbarking takes some accepting, and has astonished Europeans from David Livingstone onwards. In his *Missionary Travels* (1857), under the heading 'Vitality of the Mowana-Tree', he describes how:

'The natives make a strong cord from the fibres contained in the pounded bark.
The whole of the trunk, as high as they can reach, is consequently often quite denuded of
its covering, which in the case of almost any other tree would cause its death, but this has
no effect on the mowana except to make it throw out a new bark, which is done in the way
of granulation. This stripping of the bark is repeated frequently, so that it is common to see
the lower five or six feet an inch or two less in diameter than the parts above.'

Beneath the grey layer of outer bark, past the green chlorophyll, is the inner paler fibre, which has more uses than a ball of string. This is removed in strips, and moistened (sometimes by chewing), then pounded, before being twisted together into cords of varying thickness. Robust individuals of several tree species can occasionally survive ringbarking, but the ability of *Adansonia digitata* to tolerate the repeated removal of wide encircling panels makes it unique in Africa.

The Kenyan National Archives has a fascinating exchange of correspondence concerning the use of baobab parts. It begins in 1917 with the Conservator of Forests writing to the Colony's Acting Chief Secretary, suggesting rules be promulgated for the protection of baobabs on Crown Land. The letter is copied to the Provincial Commissioner in Mombasa, who adds: 'I now observe that natives are also removing the bark from these trees and would ask that any such Rule should contain provision for the preventing of such removal.' Back and forth go official missives between coast and capital until reason ultimately prevails and the suggestion is turned down, influenced perhaps by the Commissioner of Police noting that '... it would be only fair if the headmen were told to tell all their villagers before any action is taken; the custom of cutting bark is of long standing'.

The inhabitants of coastal Kenya were apparently twisting short lengths of cord to bundle up firewood and personal belongings. Elsewhere, thin strips of woven bark were making fishing lines, nets and strings for bows or musical instruments. In his 1863 *Journal of the Discovery of the Source of the Nile*, Captain James Grant refers to 'rope and kilts' being made from baobab bark.

Almost everywhere baobabs grow, their bark is stripped and plaited. The twisted fibres of baobab bark harness donkeys, mules or oxen to their carts, while thicker bundles make ropes with which the Dogon people in Mali haul their dead into burial caves on the cliff side. The cord itself can be woven into mats, and if the weave is tight enough the fibre can be used to make cups and other containers for liquid. Cord can also be turned into coarse cloth, waterproof hats in Senegal, fabric for shoes in Zanzibar, or fibre filters for sieving traditional honey brew elsewhere in Tanzania.

The Wakamba in Kenya hoist up beehives and lower down containers of honey with baobab bark ropes, and also make particularly fine baskets

Bark from bigger trees is often stripped off in panels. The marks on this baobab near Mwingi in Kenya show it to have a long history of providing bark for the local community.

called kiondos. They prefer to harvest fibres from young trees, small enough to be encircled with the arms of a single adult. Fibres are usually stripped off in metre lengths, and are separated from the outer bark by pounding them with the same large pestle that crushes grain.

In 2002 I met Rosemary Syungo Mwenbakau, the chairlady of the Mitamisyi Location basket-making group in central Kenya's Mwingi District. The group weaves baskets from baobab yarn and sells them through marketing centres established by various aid organizations. To make the yarn, Syungo has her children chew the strips of fibre to

This basket was made by Rosemary Syungo Mwenbakau using baobab yarn. Some of the colours are natural; others are obtained from soot and dyes.

Skilled basket makers can weave as they walk.

moisten them; once these are soft and pliable she rolls one length with another on her thigh, and in that way makes up long, easily portable, skeins.

Natural fibres vary in colour from dark brown, through pink to straw. Syungo showed me how fibres could be blackened by rubbing them in soot on the bottom of a clay cooking pot. Deep dark red colour used to be obtained from stones in the distant Tana River; but now weavers find it easier to extract the pigment by boiling up roots and dark-coloured chips of wood.

With the arrival of Europeans in Africa, human impact on many natural resources shifted from traditional, sustainable harvest to mechanized over-exploitation. Trees that had once provided local communities with food, shelter or medicine were suddenly in demand for use in a previously inconceivable range of goods for Western markets. It was fortunate for the baobab that its bark could be harvested without long-term damage to the trees because the fibre proved a popular ingredient in a particularly eclectic list of products. Before the advent of the breech-loading rifle, plugs of baobab wood were apparently in use as wadding in muzzle-loaders. The 1908 *Bulletin of Miscellaneous Information* from the Royal Botanical Gardens at Kew reported baobab being used in Angola for 'sacking and wrappers . . . for the conveyance of

Many Australian boabs eventually become hollow, just like their African congeners, and some have also been used as gaols.

The only limits to the uses for hollow baobabs are the boundaries of human imagination.

cotton, gum, copal, and orchella weed'; in India for elephant saddles; and elsewhere for helmets, caps and ladies' hats.

If the traditional harvest of bark never posed a threat to the health of local baobab populations, the same certainly could not be said for the appetite of the paper industry, particularly in South Africa. Pulp came from the wood of the baobab, rather than its bark, and this of course meant cutting down the tree. The paper was used to print Indian currency, and served as rough packaging in England. Only the difficulties of bleaching and water extraction saved the tree trunks from ending up in a far wider range of paper products. It took a public outcry from both within and without South Africa to force the legislation, which, in 1941, finally protected baobabs from the country's paper mills.

High moisture content has spared baobabs from far more than being pressed into paper. Above all it makes the wood all but useless as firewood, charcoal or building material. When a baobab finally collapses and starts to crumble, the rotting fibres make an excellent fertilizer to spread back on the land from which the tree emerged, but such benefit is certainly not enough to justify the effort of actually felling a tree.

A hollow trunk

Besides the bark, the greatest attribute of a baobab tree trunk is its emptiness. In the daily grind of rural life, the opportunity to use empty baobab trunks as stores or shelters is far too valuable to ignore. Whatever the availability of branches, skins, dung or earth, constructing shelter in Africa consumes time, energy, resources and sometimes money. Baobabs are often hollow by a relatively early age, and the ready-to-inhabit, waterproof refuges they provide seldom pass unappreciated. The eventual uses to which these natural havens are put depends on the immediate needs of the community, influenced perhaps by prevailing systems of tribal land ownership.

Ibn Battuta was inspired as much by the hollowness of the baobabs he saw in the Kingdom of Mali in 1353 as by their size, passing one where there was '. . . a man inside weaving; he had set up his loom and was weaving. I was amazed at him'. More often, hollow baobabs make homes, shops and storage space for everything from road-mending tools and bicycles to animal feed. Some hollow baobabs have doubled as stables, meeting places and a dairy, and trees growing beside well-travelled roads are likely to serve as bus shelters. The baobab at Duiwelskloof is now fitted out as

a watering hole for human visitors, and another South African tree was used as a beer store for a nearby bar known as the Murchison Club.

Local administrations in remote areas without prisons have sometimes incarcerated offenders in baobab trunks, both in Australia and Africa. Immediately outside the police station in Kasane, in northeastern Botswana, stands an ancient baobab. Partially collapsed, in 2004 the tree was proudly floodlit notwithstanding, or possibly even because of, its history as the women's prison. Round the back of the police station was another baobab, its tiny, easily blocked hole also fitting the tree ideally for use as a prison. My policewoman guide seemed embarrassed by its history, but somehow reassured by the presence of a basket in the entrance, in which dozed a yellow and black lizard next to a folded square of paper. With Botswana having the highest AIDS infection rates in the world, was this a cry for help from one of the sufferers?

Further north, in Katima Mulilo, on the banks of the Zambezi, grows one of the most renowned baobabs on the African continent, converted with some ingenuity, but wanton disrespect, into a flush lavatory. The tree is on a road junction in the old administrative centre, next door to the local SWAPO office, from which loud Lingala music was blaring when I called by. The baobab's expanding roots had wedged the door immovably ajar, allowing anyone to see inside, but not enter. Sometime over the last two years the door has been removed.

Elsewhere around what is now northern Botswana, baobabs served as informal postboxes. Hunters, prospectors, missionaries and others living on the edge of the Kalahari wastes would leave their correspondence in the tree for passers-by heading for South Africa to post there. Likewise, anyone travelling north would collect

The famous tree in Katima Mulilo, which was converted into a flush lavatory; with the door wedged shut its only practical use in 2004 was to advertise the forthcoming Namibian elections.

This baobab near Salaita Hill in Kenya is said to have provided the hideout for a German sniper during World War I.

soldiers from the rear. This much is fact, but at least some of what comes next may be the product of an urge not to let the truth get in the way of a good story.

Attached to the Allied troops were local Wakamba askaris who, for reasons long forgotten, had been banned from taking snuff. They knew the sniper's hideout, or so the story goes, but refused to reveal it so long as the ban continued. Reluctantly, the officers relented, whereupon the askaris lifted their arms together and all pointed to a distant baobab. When the soldiers finally surrounded the sniper's refuge, they found a woman inside.

The tree is easy to find, and has a gaping hole in the top of the trunk where the branches

Many wells make use of the hollow trunk of the boabab, but here the cavity left by the rotted root has created water storage capacity.

mail for those same lonely migrants, and drop it in the baobab poste restante for collection.

Salaita Hill, near Taveta in southern Kenya, was the scene of one of many actions fought by the elusive German general, Paul von Lettow-Vorbeck, to tie down vastly superior numbers of Allied troops during World War I. The hill guarded the strategically important Taveta Gap through the line of mountains running east from Kilimanjaro. In the dry February heat of 1916, South African soldiers were struggling to dislodge the Germans from their entrenched positions on the slopes. Time after time they were repulsed, and to compound their casualties, a hidden sniper kept picking off fork. I jumped down into the hollow to look for bullet cases, and to imagine this unlikely fighter crouched there for days on end, victualled, so they say, by faithful Taveta retainers. The story has many different endings: that she was blasted by shell fire, shot resisting capture, or taken prisoner. Variations on the theme add a father into the tree; others more romantically suggest she was avenging the death of a German lover. Eventually, the general withdrew, almost vaporizing, as he so often did. That, too, is fact, but nowhere have I been able to find the identity of this Valkyrie, nor whose soul she would sweep off to Valhalla.

Not only the living, but also the dead found shelter in baobabs, and in Senegal hollow trunks were the final resting places for the bodies of some of the Serer people. Alive, *griots* were semi-outcasts, which, as musicians, clowns, fortune-tellers, general entertainers, gurus and professional praise-singers to the famous, seems particularly unfair. Somehow, their fellow human beings seemed unable to accept and absorb them into normal life – or normal death. For *griots*, the final resting place was a hollow baobab, their enshrouded bodies suspended inside the trunk, or piled up in heaps in the empty trees, slowly mummifying. These peculiar burial rites may survive in remote areas, but mostly live on only in anthropological papers, the memories of tribal elders and the memoirs of French colonial administrators.

The living human body is best nurtured by hollow baobabs when they fill up with water. It seems strange that the use of hollow trunks as wells is not nearly as widespread as the trees are. Obviously use is fuelled by necessity and in those blessed pockets of baobab-strewn Africa with no serious shortage of water, its storage is of little concern. But where most baobabs grow, water is scarce, and maintaining a supply throughout the dry times may literally be a matter of life and death.

In the absence of cement, corrugated iron or a good hole in the ground, baobabs make extremely effective wells, and if nature does not hollow them out, man is perfectly able to do so himself.

The best-known baobab wells are those in Kordofan in central Sudan, where baobabs are known by the Berber name *tebeldi*. Old age often hollows out the trees naturally, otherwise Hamar tribesmen excavate the centres with axes and knives, causing no more apparent injury to the baobab's wellbeing than do human bark strippers or stressed elephants. The process is well described in the *Geographical Journal* (1910) by Captain Watkiss Lloyd, one-time governor of Kordofan:

'The baobab trees have to be carefully prepared for use as reservoirs. The large branches are first cut off near the trunk. If this is not done, the trunk is apt to split as soon as it is hollowed out. A hole is cut in the trunk, generally just above a branch, which serves as a platform for the man who is filling the tree, and the interior is hollowed out. Round the bottom of the tree a shallow basin some 20 or 30 feet in diameter is made, in which the rain-water collects. As soon as there is a storm, the people go out and fill their trees. The water so stored remains perfectly good until the end of the next hot weather, or even longer. A few trees, naturally hollow, have a hole at the top between the branches, and fill themselves, the branches catching the water and acting as gutters. These are called "lagai" and are highly valued by the Hamars.'

Hadzabe honey hunters near Lake Eyasi in Tanzania move up a baobab tree by hammering successive hardwood pegs into the trunk.

These *tebeldis* play a crucial role in Sudanese society. Nowhere are there likely to have been enough natural baobab wells to sustain permanent settlement, and, until people began hollowing out the trees artificially, most of Kordofan would only have supported nomads. It is not an exaggeration to say that many villages only exist because nearby baobabs store water through the dry months. Long-term settlements quickly degrade marginal land, and the wells quite possibly end up watering more people than the land itself is capable of supporting.

Tebeldis have enormous value in areas where the notion of private landownership prevails, and can be sold, argued about, fought over, or handed down from one generation to the next like ancestral heirlooms. Each district has a register of wells in which they are noted and named. Many are prefaced with *Um*, Arabic for mother, followed by a word connected with water or some other marked characteristic of the particular tree. *Um Dhirifa* means 'the tearful', which may allude to the tree's leaking, and *Um Laqui* (anglicized to 'lagai' above) are the wells that fill naturally. *Um Asal* refers to the honey in the tree and *Um Tiyur* is the home of birds.

While the dependence on baobab wells in Kordofan is almost unique, the tree's natural capacity to store water has certainly not been lost on the inhabitants of other parts of Africa. Ibn Battuta remarked on baobabs in 14th century Mali that collected drinkable water, and itinerant Bushmen in Namibia and Botswana still rely on baobab cisterns to help them travel through the otherwise waterless wastes of the Kalahari. The Bushmen suck the water from the bottom of tree cisterns through long straws made out of interconnected reeds – 'sipping sticks'.

ABOVE: Bees are encouraged to inhabit artificial hives if there are not enough natural nesting places for them. Honey is usually harvested at night, hives first being lowered to the ground and the bees stupefied by smoke.
OVERLEAF: Shade from the midday African sun is one of the greatest benefits any big tree can grant to man or animal.

Bees in trees

Hollows in branches are often taken over by bees, and all over Africa, wooden pegs on baobab trunks lead up to their nests. The pegs are made of ebony, *Combretum* or other hard wood, and often outlast the tenure of the bees. These prongs linger on, as much part of the tree's history as the elephant scars on its bark. If bees need further encouragement, or more appealing nest sites, artificial hives are suspended from the baobab's great spreading branches, sometimes hanging all over the tree like a crop of giant oblong fruit.

The branches have been cut off this Eritrean tree so that leaves can be fed to livestock and, possibly, to humans too. Ideally, leaves are harvested without cutting branches because fewer branches means fewer flowers and so less fruit.

The most enthusiastic beekeepers in Kenya are the Wakamba, much of whose homeland is populated with baobabs. They hollow out *Commiphora* branches to make hives, closing them with lids at either end and chipping out a small entrance hole in the bottom. To attract bees, hives are smeared inside with beeswax and aromatic leaves, then hoisted up into the branches. Having adopted a hive, the bees then begin breeding, successive generations sometimes occupying the same one for 15 years or more.

Bees nesting naturally in baobabs do so because of the hole, not because the tree offers any particular biological or chemical attraction. Apart from the baobabs' size and their magnificent spreading branches, which are ideal for hanging hives from, the Wakamba also like the trees for their smooth bark. This makes them difficult for honey badgers to climb. These powerful creatures are completely fearless, and their lust for honey is so strong they will attack dogs, and even humans, in the way. Once up the tree, honey badgers raid any hives within reach, and access others by gnawing off branches or ropes, then breaking open the fallen hives on the ground.

A hundred other uses

Supporting the baobab's massive bulk is a shallow network of roots. The bark on the bigger roots can be twisted into ropes, much as can that on the trunk, and the hole left by the roots of a fallen tree sometimes makes a water store. There seems to be enough nutrition – and an almond-like taste – in the thinner, terminal roots for these to be worth simmering and chewing in times of real food shortages. Seedling roots are much more tender and their seasonal scarcity makes them something of a delicacy, particularly the swollen, radish-like taproot.

Leaves, flowers and fruit on the tree nourish different birds and animals. Herbivores graze the leaves if they can reach them, antelopes and livestock nibble fallen petals, and baboons crack open the pods and swallow the contents. Birds probe around the flowers for nectar, insects invade the fallen fruit, and smaller mammals scurry off into the undergrowth with seeds. Small wonder, therefore, that omnivorous man also finds baobab produce the source of much goodness.

The knowledge that parts of certain plants are palatable may be inherited or learnt, or perhaps even acquired in more ethereal ways. To keep knowledge alive it needs to be used, and fundamental to knowing how to use any particular plant is its presence. Yet even where baobabs grow, the knowledge of this goodness is often ignored.

Most of those living around baobab trees know that the leaves make good eating. 'Good' is relative, and in the more fertile parts of baobab country local inhabitants seldom resort to eating baobab leaves or feeding them to livestock, and the trees retain the full-branched look, quite unlike those in Eritrea or the Sahel. There the annual harvest of greenery stunts baobab limbs, and is bought at the price of far fewer fruit from these pollarded trees.

Leaves are at their tastiest and most nutritious when they are pale greeny-yellow, tender, soft and small. They can then be eaten straight or boiled up and added to soup. My first efforts at cooking baobab foliage met with little success as I watched my guests shovelling forkfuls of greenery into their mouths before awkwardly removing long stringy fibres, like the ribs of old French beans. Only once I began pulling the two halves of the leaf off their central ribs before cooking was this spinach-like delicacy truly appreciated.

Fresh leaves adorn market stalls for very few months, and to make the supply of leaves last through the year they must be dried, then stored, either in powdered form or whole. Leaves dry quickly and easily in the sun, but this destroys their carotene which is a source of vitamin A. It is better to dry them slowly in the shade. In the language of the Wolof people of Senegal, powdered leaves are known as *lalo*, and there, as elsewhere, used to season and thicken stews, make sauces and add to couscous or local porridge. Like baobab fruit, the fresh leaves are rich in vitamin C, most of which is lost once these are dried, although drying enhances calcium content.

And when even dried food is running out, fresh baobab blooms will not be ignored, if not as a source of food, then at the very least as a flavour for drinks.

A mix of pollen and water makes a reasonable glue, and the woman who owns the Baobab Café in the Old Town of Zanzibar remembers creating dolls out of baobab flowers, petals making up the skirts and stamens the hair. Sometimes she would spend hours plucking pollen from the stamens, and end by whispering to her flower-doll, 'Pretty baby, your hair is now clean'.

If bats or bushbabies have done their work, small fruit will start appearing on the ends of the baobab branches, where the flowers once were, slowly enlarging over the coming months. By the time the seeds are ripe, embedded in their white acidic pith, the tree is usually leafless, dripping with the baubles of hard-shelled pods.

This Tanzanian may have put these pods aside to sell later, because no trees seemed to be fruiting anywhere nearby from which he could have harvested fresh ones.

The pith's most notorious component is its vitamin C (ascorbic acid). Different analyses report it to be anything between four and ten times richer in vitamin C than are oranges. All agree it is the richest known natural source of the vitamin, which promotes healing and is particularly important for healthy bones and tendons. The pith also contains tartaric acid, sometimes called cream of tartar. Added to baking powder, this is the extract from potassium bitartrate for which baobab fruit pith has often been used as a substitute – not least in the field kitchens of both British and German armies during World War I.

The baobab pith's vitamin C content is probably the most important reason for the tree's dispersal round the Indian Ocean coast, as well as over to the West Indies. On long sea journeys fruit would have provided a perfect source of vitamin C, easily stored, long lasting, a powerful antidote to scurvy that was ignored by the British navy.

Scurvy is a result of vitamin C deficiency, and takes around six months to manifest itself. George Anson's round-the-world voyage was just one of many badly afflicted by scurvy. Starting out from England in 1740 at the head of six vessels and 2 000 men, he returned four years later with a mere 200 men in a single ship. At that point he was losing up to ten sailors a day from a disease whose symptoms were described by his chaplain, Richard Walter, as including:

'... large discoloured spots over the whole surface of the body, swelled legs, putrid gums ... extraordinary lassitude of the whole body ... ulcers of the worst kind attended with rotten bones, and such a luxuriancy of fungous flesh as yielded to no remedy.'

Dipping pith-covered seeds into a sugary dye makes them appealing sweets for children all along the East African coast.

Stocking up at one of the West African ports with baobab fruit would have saved hundreds of lives. Captain James Cook suspected that fresh vegetables kept the disease at bay during the first of his three epic voyages, in 1768, but not until 1795 were British naval ships issued with lime juice.

Repeatedly knocking pods before breaking them open, helps separate pith from seeds, otherwise this is best done by adding the pod's contents to water and stirring the mixture with a forked stick. When mixed with water or milk (which it curdles), pith produces a healthy and refreshing drink, acid tasting, rather like sherbet. This can be sweetened by adding sugar or honey, and the mixture condensed into quite an acceptable jam. Along the East African coast the pith is flavoured

Sucking these sweets and spitting out the pips may help disperse the seeds.

In eastern Kenya pith and seeds are separated by first soaking the contents of the pod in water, then agitating the mixture with a special stirring stick.

with coconut, and the mixture thickened into a sauce for enlivening maize meal, ground guinea corn or other local versions of porridge.

Where power supplies are consistent enough to keep water iced, baobab pulp, water and sugar, together with cloves or nutmeg, are frozen into a delicious sorbet-style confection. Children crowd round Malian bus stops, cold-boxes around their necks full of lollipops: red ones flavoured with hibiscus flowers, milky white ones with the pith of the baobab fruit. Seeds coated in coloured sugar are sold in packets all along the East African coast. The spat-out pips littering the pavements in Zanzibar's Stone Town are giveaway signs of a Koranic school (*madrasa*) behind the ornately carved door.

Pith smoulders slowly enough to make a good insect repellent, or to smoke fish and, perhaps inevitably, also finds its way into traditional alcohol. The Wasandawe of central Tanzania are just one of many African tribes who make a brew of baobab pith, adding water, flour and yeast.

The seeds, too, are also nutritious, rich in protein and potassium. However, to become remotely palatable they either need cooking, fermenting or at least pounding up. Roasting makes seeds brittle, and easier to grind, either to use like coffee in hot drinks or to make a culinary flavouring. If the husks can be removed, the kernels provide an excellent edible oil. They are full of fat, as well as calcium, thiamine and iron, with even more vitamin B1 than ground nuts or rice bran. Katong balls are a Ghanaian food, made by pounding fried seeds and water into a paste; this is allowed to ferment for two days before being rolled into balls and left to dry.

Mashed pips have made shampoos for Swahili women for many centuries, and throwing out the seeds after hair-washing is said to have contributed to the growth of baobabs around human settlements.

Enclosing the pith and oil-filled pips is the seed pod; the multi-shaped, all-purpose container.

impetus to such a discovery is obviously muted by the availability of alternatives. If vines grew all over baobab trees, offering long, strong stems as ready-made ropes, the potential of baobab fibre for the same purpose might still be locked up in the tree trunk. In wetter parts of the baobab's range, blessed with a greater diversity of plant life, there are more potential sources of food for humans or livestock than where the baobab protrudes almost alone out of scrubby semi-desert.

On much of the East African coast, average annual rainfall is well over 100 cm, and residents are favoured with an abundant supply of alternative sources of food. Some of them eat baobab leaves

PREVIOUS PAGES: The sea is never far away in Zanzibar, and, with a wide variety of other fruit and vegetables available, it is perhaps not surprising that local residents do very little with bark, fruit or any other baobab tree produce.
ABOVE: Empty baobab pods make rat traps on the East African coast; maize kernels lure the rodent into the trap, and nibbling at the food triggers a noose to tighten round its neck.

Old pods, still full of seeds, can make fishing floats or be rattled to the beat of traditional music, and once emptied of their natural contents the only restrictions on their uses are the limits of human imagination. This has produced flower-pots, water containers, snuff boxes, drums, carved decorations, lamp or candle shades, canoe paddles and a host of other utilitarian articles. Pods burn well, and the resulting ash, rich in potassium, makes fertilizer and soap – and if there is anything left over after all that, powdered pods are even said to be worth smoking or adding to snuff.

Necessity is the mother of invention, and surely drove the discovery of many of the benefits conferred on local communities by the baobab tree. Yet the

The curved stick forms the spring-loading that tightens the noose around the rat's neck.

All over Africa, women roll lengths of baobab fibre along their thighs, then plait them together into long lengths of cord.

Hadzabe men prefer to strip baobab bark from young branches which they first cut from high up the tree.

The contents of these seed pods have been taken away to coat with sweetener and then sell in packets to children.

and fruit pith, but generally the only serious activity around the baobab is scraping out pith-covered seeds to sweeten and sell as confectionery. Piles of red-fibred shell husks lie around the trees, seemingly not even worth taking home to burn on the stove.

In Zanzibar it is even harder to find anyone who does anything with any part of the baobab except to make bonbons (*mabuyu*). No-one even seems to mix pith into sauces or vitamin drinks. Nearly every leaf on every Zanzibari baobab sees out its full four- or five-month natural span, immune from harvest for either human or animal consumption. Compared to the harshest parts of the baobab's range, like the Sahel or northern Kalahari, most of Zanzibar is a proverbial land of milk and honey. The sea and its bounty are never far away, rain falls regularly, and at any time of year huge arrays of fruit and vegetables, all of foreign origin, are displayed on roadside stalls. This super-abundance of local produce seems to have rendered the baobab's products superfluous. Was it always so? Until the arrival of all this sustenance the baobab must surely have provided the inhabitants of Zanzibar with more than pips to suck and the odd pair of bark-rope sandals.

CHAPTER EIGHT

The healing tree

Wherever baobabs grow, they are central to traditional healing practices. Medicinal compounds are extracted from fruit, wood and leaves. The trees and the ground around them serve as stages for rituals of treatment. Baobabs are vital in sustaining local people both culturally and nutritionally. So utterly do they dominate their landscapes, and so long do they endure, it takes no great leap of belief to revere them as homes of spirits or at least conduits to the ethereal world beyond. Animists still imbue the tree with its own spirit. Other Africans, whose spiritual lives also remain uncluttered by the strictures of modern religion, find the base of a huge baobab somewhere to pray to a god that may be everywhere, but is surely more there than anywhere else.

A tree of hope

Kenyatta Drive runs along the more developed length of the seafront in Dar es Salaam. In the garden of Number 12, where Roald Dahl once lived, is a gigantic baobab, so huge that the plot's perimeter wall curves to accommodate the trunk. On the other side of the road is a much smaller baobab on a piece of open grassland, above low coral cliffs dropping down to the beach. The smaller tree is studded with thousands of dhow nails, each of which once fixed a prayer or talisman to the trunk.

These pleas were written on folded squares of paper, and, when I was there, the more recent ones had still not disintegrated in the tropical monsoon storms. Some of the nails impaled objects used in the course of tree-side ceremonies. From a branch hung a black bag, spiked with protruding porcupine quills, the dried skin of a puffer fish swung in the wind, and ragged bits of cloth fluttered from twigs and trunk like Buddhist prayer flags.

So many dreams, prayers, great hopes and much disappointment were all bound up in the hapless baobab. The tree itself seemed to suffer neither from the burden of so much collective expectation, nor from serving as a giant pincushion. It was not yet large enough to generate the particular reverence accorded huge and ancient trees, and no-one I spoke to referred to this baobab's supernatural attributes. Rather, it was a tree accessible to all, and so provided a stage for rituals of healing and help.

PREVIOUS PAGES: Religion and animism seem to meet in this shrine of tree and coral rock in Mocimboa in northern Mozambique.
ABOVE: This tree grows in Dar es Salaam and features in ceremonies of prayer and healing. The sea is not only a cleanser, but also an acceptable resting place for cast-out spirits.

The trunk of the healing tree in Dar es Salaam into which thousands of dhow nails have been hammered, some of which affixed prayers and others pieces of clothing or fetishes.

One sticky afternoon, the tree's magnetic promise drew two Swahili women to its shelter. I assumed them to be mother and daughter, shepherded by an African man who was clearly a traditional healer. The girl sat down, her legs out towards the trunk, while the other two fussed around her. The man began applying a floury white powder to the girl's face, and the mother then passed her hands seven times around her daughter's head. After more ceremony and loud incantations, the healer took a thin strip of bark from the tree and tied it to the girl's hair – an amulet against continued infertility? Shortly after they had left, a ragged youth bore his troubles to the tree, alone. He left an offering to his god – broken coconut, bottles of dark red liquid, and a bright red cloak. The act of breaking the coconut may have been symbolic of the release of evil from his system.

Since that day I have been back to that baobab only once. I took a taxi from the airport and asked the driver to park nearby while I wandered and watched. He refused to wait for me near the tree; there were many disturbed spirits around it, cast out during healing rituals and searching for new corporeal resting places. Even if it meant losing a fare, this was one risk he was not prepared to take.

A tradition of healing

Traditional healing in Africa seldom distinguishes between treatment of mind or body, irrespective of which the sickness is apparently afflicting. Illness is seen as striking at both, or being caused by an imbalance of one manifesting itself in a disturbance of the other. To treat the body in isolation, as western allopathic medicine does, is almost inconceivable. Traditional treatment entails the prescription of medicine, but it places far greater stress on a psychological approach to its administration. Traditional healing is also a much more personal practice, individual practitioners bringing to the medicine itself, or to its application, their own idiosyncratic contributions.

Nonetheless, the subjective nature of traditional treatment should not detract from the fundamental and well-accepted medicinal properties of various parts of different plants. Some of these properties are so widely recognized as to be common to the whole continent; others are confined to a single tribal area.

The Poacher's Hideout in Tarangire shows a bare silhouette in the dry season.

Any body of traditional medicinal knowledge has accumulated in many different ways, not least through a multi-generational process of trial, observation and maybe disastrous error, before remedies finally receive general acceptance. An awareness of some of the medicinal or nutritional benefits of baobab fruit may be inherited, even from before we stood up. Other wisdom could have been received by shamans while in altered states of consciousness, and then handed down to practitioners of traditional healing.

Near Mtwara, in southern Tanzania, I talked with several *waganga* – a Swahili word for those who treat sickness with a combination of traditional medicinal remedies and psychological witchcraft. They all prescribed a toothache treatment derived from baobab sap, and one of them advised his patients to rub themselves all over with a similar

Baobabs in the dry and rainy seasons look so different, they almost look like different species. This lush baobab is the same Tarangire tree as that shown above, but just after the rains.

decoction to restore flagging vitality – a procedure he vividly enacted down to the removal of all his clothes except a pair of tartan underpants. Beyond this, the baobab had no medicinal properties of which any of them was aware, although the trees or their parts played an important role in the more ceremonial aspects of their craft.

Further north in Tanzania, many Hadzabe hunter-gatherers will say that they have no medicinal use for any part of the baobab, other than the pith, which they eat more as food than medicine. Not even their gods are connected with the trees, but rather the sun and the moon. The Hadzabe live impoverished lives, surviving exclusively on what they can gather from their environment, and their minimal use of the baobab's resources is astonishing. Elsewhere, particularly in West Africa, the position is dramatically different, and the lush chemical factory of the tree in full leaf is an irresistible source of nutritional, medicinal or spiritual benefit.

Arboreal pharmacy

The leaves alone are almost a panacea for the ills of the surrounding communities, with healers and mothers applying them to patients or children as emollients, tranquillizers and astringents. Rich in calcium and vitamin A, the leaves also treat diarrhoea, dysentery, asthma, colic, eye infections, general fatigue, fever, inflammations, earache, kidney problems, urinary infections, insect bites, digestive and respiratory problems, sweating, tumours and wounds.

Concoctions of powdered leaves are used as antihistamines, expectorants and diaphoretics to promote sweating. Powdered leaves (*lalo*) are a staple in the diets of many West Africans, who believe these also help cleanse their blood. Baobab leaves are used both to treat malaria, and as a prophylactic against the illness.

External wounds are treated with leaf poultices, which are believed by northern Nigerians to help heal the wounds of circumcision. Livingstone cured skin ulcers with poultices of baobab leaf powder. These sores may have erupted through lack of vitamin C, and it is quite possible that once his expedition came across baobab trees, its members also ate the vitamin-rich pith from the seed pod, thus stimulating the healing process from within.

The bark has a very bitter taste and was once used commercially for treating fevers, under the Latin name *cortex cael cedra* – 'heavenly blue bark'. A decoction is used to bathe children with rickets and other weaknesses, and added to steam baths to control shivering, colds and flu. Over much of the continent it makes a mouthwash for toothache sufferers, and in parts of Tanzania boiled bark peelings are used to treat stomach ache and general body pains. A tasteless and insoluble gum can be extracted from the sap and applied to cleanse wounds and sores.

The oily red mush of pounded *Strophanthus* seeds is one of many lethal poisons with which

The pith surrounding baobab seeds is almost universally appreciated as a food and medicine wherever the trees grow; its vitamin C both prevents and cures disease.

Bushmen and other hunters in southern Africa tip their arrows. Most poison users have developed an antidote to the lethal effects of their toxic arrow tips, and for the Bushmen this is found in baobab seeds. The active ingredient is an alkaloid, traces of which are also found in the bark. In Malawi it is juices from the trunk, rather than the seeds, that are smeared around the wounds of animals killed with poisoned arrows to neutralize the toxin before consuming the kill.

In South Africa, many local people were said to use the powdered seeds to stop children hiccoughing, while both seeds and pith treat dysentery in Central Africa. The seeds can also be ground into a paste for massaging onto sore teeth and gums, and, in other parts of the continent, for easing gastric and kidney complaints, and aching joints. The paste may be swallowed or applied externally, and the Wakamba in Kenya first make incisions around the infected area before rubbing it into the skin.

The white pith encasing the seeds treats malaria and other fevers, and is used to revive weakened children. Vitamin C is an aid to general good health, and it is easy to understand how soup or sauce made from the pith would promote general wellbeing, acting both to prevent and cure diseases. In some parts of Africa the pith is used as a disinfectant, and in others as a dysentery treatment, while its use as a cure for measles and smallpox seems widespread.

Even roots have their uses, and can be soaked in water and used to bathe babies in order to strengthen their immunity. Like other parts of the tree, powdered roots are said to make an effective treatment for malaria. Healers also apply concoctions containing baobab roots to relieve general lassitude, as well as impotence, alleviating the one no doubt going a long way towards curing the other.

The roots of treatment

Theoretically, similar uses of the same raw materials in different parts of the world could derive from traditional practices inherited from a common ancestor. However, in many cases this idea raises far more questions than it answers. The Tanzanian Hadzabe have a very similar click language to that of the Bushmen in Namibia and Botswana, and both live hunter-gatherer lives around baobab trees. Yet while they may share distant ancestors, my hope of discovering they also share some particularly esoteric usage of baobab parts was not realized.

On the other hand, completely unrelated tribal groups, separated by several thousand miles of African savanna or forest, sometimes reach similar ethnobotanical conclusions. The Wakamba are the only people in East Africa recorded as using juice from baobab leaves to cure infected eyes. In Senegal, young stems are crushed to provide a similar treatment. Local tribesfolk in parts of Kenya have found that baobab roots made a good red dye, as they also have in Gambia.

Fundamentally, common usage must derive from parallel responses to similar needs, pressures and ideas. Add to that the fact that the most obvious way to gain knowledge is from others who already have it. Appreciation of the particular medicinal properties of plants is often regional rather than tribal and unless there was a dramatic language barrier, it is likely that knowledge, however acquired, diffused into surrounding areas. The benefits accruing from eating pith from the pod are known throughout the continent, and even the baobab bark toothache treatment is almost Africa-wide. Sometimes, though, knowledge seems strangely restricted. Are the Giriama the only ones to dig out pieces of the central tap root of younger trees to make a decoction with which to treat blood disorders?

ABOVE: This intricately decorated baobab pod has a variety of ceremonial uses for the Dogon people in Mali.
OVERLEAF: Over most of its range, much more sustainable use could be made of the baobab; sheep and goats will greedily eat young leaves if these are harvested for them.

Why does smouldering pith not keep insects off children's faces or leftover food in more of the continent than it does?

Just as the availability of alternatives regulates the importance of baobab leaves as a source of nourishment for humans or their livestock, so it must presumably affect the extent to which medicinal use is made of baobab parts. One can only assume that, presented with a baobab in all its seasonal glories, it is having the choice of so much other suitable vegetation that has kept the local people in much of East Africa from feeding baobab leaves to children or livestock. In *Useful Plants of Ghana*, Daniel Abbiw points to over 70 different herbal remedies for toothache, which can be gargled, chewed, swallowed, sucked, or made into ointments and mouthwashes. Baobab bark decoction is just one of the 70, which must speak loudly about the reliance on any one treatment diminishing in the face of available alternatives.

Madagascar's first human inhabitants most likely arrived less than 2 000 years ago, to an ethnobotanically blank slate. Most of them came from the east, Polynesia or Malaya, where nothing like baobabs existed. Having no relationship with the island's bizarre vegetation, they must have relied initially on trial and error (or, perhaps, carefully studying the habits of wild animals) to discover what was good for them.

Hungry immigrants would quickly have discovered that the pulp of baobab fruit was both palatable and non-poisonous, even if the true nutritional worth took longer to appreciate, and now the fruit is a valuable supplement to a lot of impoverished diets of fish and rice. Being sailors, early settlers would also have wasted no time in searching for barks, vines and other rope-twisting fibres. How long was it before they started using the inner bark from the huge cylindrical trunks of *Adansonia grandidieri*? Recognizing the more abstruse medicinal properties of baobabs would have come less easily to the immigrants and in distant rural areas of Madagascar the inhabitants may still be in the learning stage. There are very few records of any medicinal usage beyond the preparation from the bark of the very localized *A. suarezensis* as a treatment for diabetes.

Aborigines have been in Australia at least ten times longer than anyone has inhabited Madagascar. This, and the scarcity of natural resources over much of the land they call home, seems to have fomented a deeper affinity with their environment than exists among the Malagasy, who appear more determined to destroy their botanical inheritance than preserve it. Like anyone else around a baobab tree, Aborigines eat fruit pulp, either dry or mixed into a soup, and also make use of the seeds – raw, roasted, baked or ground into a paste. While Thomas Baines was in Australia in 1855 on the North Australia Exploring Expedition, he described curing scurvy by feeding sailors a jam of boab fruit and sugar, presumably a treatment grounded in Aboriginal practice. Baines also followed the indigenous inhabitants in chewing wood for its moisture. Feeding boab leaves to cattle, as Aborigines do, mirrors the practice in Africa; so does stripping the inner bark fibres and, after pounding them with rocks, rolling them into lengths of string. Producing a sort of super-glue from boab pollen, strong enough to fix the metal heads to spear shafts, also has parallels in Africa.

Believing

Considered as a pan-African resource, baobabs are underutilized, and in much of the continent fruit and foliage could both be sustainably exploited far more than they are. Perhaps unfortunately, though, while science endorses many of the traditionally recognized properties

A *mganga* prepares his patient for a healing session before this tree in Dar es Salaam. The woman came to the tree with her husband, and the ceremony ended with her smashing a coconut on the rock in front of the tree.

of the tree's parts, quantities of active ingredients are insufficient for fruit or leaves to be worth harvesting commercially. Such medicinal benefits as the baobab might theoretically have to offer First World sufferers seem to be better extracted from other plants with more potent chemical make-ups. Half a century ago, scientific researchers experimented with an extract from baobab leaves they called Adansonin, getting as far as giving the formula for this concoction an identification number – $C48\ H36\ O33$. This is about as close as the baobab has ever got to conferring mass medicinal benefits on the western world, although

it has not escaped the rush by pharmaceutical or beauty product companies to try and patent some of the natural remedies it offers.

Irrespective of the ingredients in traditional herbal medicines, the ritual surrounding the treatment can be crucial to its success. This is epitomized in the practice of the East Africa *mganga*. He, or less often she, may be any combination of doctor, apothecary, priest, soothsayer, spirit medium, shaman, even magician or hypnotist, and treatments almost always combine elements of the psychological and physiological. The idea of transferring sickness, or using trees or other

Ninety-year-old Namari Godogo is a Taneka healer and rainmaker; he receives visitors and patients in front of this baobab in his village in Benin.

natural or personal objects as channels through which illness can be released, is a common component of traditional healing. In Tanzania I met a local Makonde with an open suppurating wound on his leg, who had eventually decided to visit the *mganga*. With much ceremony, the healer had massaged ointment all over the wound, and then, pulling a twig from out of his bag of talismans, had directed the limping patient to rub this around the wound. With the twig well soaked with juices from the sore, the patient was told to stick it into a baobab tree, which would then absorb the sickness.

It is probably impossible to dissociate the truly pharmacological benefits of traditional treatment from the psychological effects of the ceremony surrounding it. *Jinns* (djinnis, jinnis or genies) are spirits, sometimes evil and often inspired by fertile, and fearful, imaginations. Traditional doctors can influence these imaginations, perhaps by embroidering the existence of jinns to such an extent that the medicinal treatment becomes almost irrelevant compared to the manipulations of the mind.

Infertile women can be cruelly stigmatized in African society, and their problems account for a large part of any *mganga's* business. When visited by a patient for the first time, a Wakamba witch doctor may shake his gourd full of rattling trinkets. If seven baobab seeds tumble out onto the earthen floor of the hut, the patient – man or woman – is seen to be under a spell preventing him or her from having children. To lift the spell, the doctor takes baobab fibre rope, anoints it with a combination of powders and potions, and ties seven knots along its length. He then holds the rope over the patient's head and pulls hard on each end, undoing the knots. Fertility is then assured. This may be one man's treatment, but inevitably one is left wondering whether any of it is common to other healers, or whether it is entirely the fruit of his own inventiveness or imagination.

Some years ago, I talked to an old Makonde medicine man called Mayunga. He was happy to discuss his practice – but only after being presented with clothes or bags of fruit. After talking through our interpreter (the local teacher) for half an hour, he started slowing down and the answers came with increasing reluctance. This was not, I was told, because he was tired, but rather that I had exhausted the worth of my gifts, and he expected more to continue disclosing his secrets. Mayunga was like a jukebox that needed feeding with money to get music, but his music was sweet. His particular baobab shrine of healing was in the middle of a sisal plantation. He would give patients a clay pot, full of medicine, and direct them to the tree. There they should empty the contents over their naked bodies, alone, before smashing the pot at their feet. When I visited the tree, shards of broken pot littered the ground, witness to his popularity as a healer.

Richest of all Mayunga's stories, worth bags more avocados than I had with me, was the revelation of his supernatural powers. As a youth, working on a Tanzanian sisal plantation, he was told one day to cut down a baobab. He spent six hours chopping away at the tree knowing it would take three days to fell. Next day he returned to his work, only to find an untouched trunk, showing no signs of the previous day's damage. Again Mayunga set to, piles of wood chips slowly collecting at his feet as he hacked his way round the spongy bole. The following morning he again found the baobab unharmed and entire, so went and told his employer he neither would nor could cut down the tree. Unsurprisingly he was sacked, and the job given to his brother, Alambalamba, who duly toppled the giant, but immediately fell very sick. The Makonde have long believed that cutting a baobab will make your neck stiffen rigidly at right angles, which was just what happened to Alambalamba. Mayunga visited his brother and felt as soon as he walked into the darkened room

In some cultures felling a baobab is inconceivable, for fear of dislodging the spirits that live there, but these Wakamba in Kenya were happy to sacrifice the tree for more building space.

that he would be able to loosen his neck, which he did. This first recognition of his own spiritual strength he attributed to the tree he could not kill, and he has revered baobabs ever since.

Today, many herbal medicines are sold from conventional pharmacies to be taken without any particular ceremony. Always critical to a medicine's success in healing is the patient's confidence in the treatment. Men who become strong and virile from drinking water mixed with baobab sap do so through the strength of their belief in the remedy as much as because of the medical properties of the tree. However, in South Africa babies too young to formulate such notions are washed in the mixture to strengthen their immunity, so its efficacy must rely on something other than any psychological impact of the treatment on the patient. West African fishermen rinse themselves down with an infusion of baobab seeds to protect against crocodile attacks. This presumably induces a crocodile-repelling aroma in the skin, which could perhaps be scientifically identified. Still, one should not deride the notion that beliefs can be strong enough to influence not only the believers, but also the behaviour of animals or other people with whom they interact.

Sacred trees and spirits

While trees often become focal points for public prayer and healing, seldom are they formally consecrated as places of worship as is a baobab at Keren, a beautiful mountain-ringed town in northern Eritrea. There, in 1881, a hollow baobab was dedicated as a shrine to the Virgin Mary. It is a peaceful place, approached along an avenue of neem trees (*Azadirachta indica*), and the statue of the Virgin inside is unusual for her blackness. As refuges and homes for so many wild creatures, baobabs would seem to make more appropriate

human sanctuaries than sniper's platforms, and, while Allied forces bombarded Keren from the surrounding mountains in World War II, Italian soldiers sheltered in the baobab shrine. What are described as shrapnel marks are still visible today. The tree's adoption by the Roman Catholic church seems to have enhanced its appeal to anyone in need of spiritual revitalization, and many of its visitors go there for the sanctity and tranquillity of the place, as much as for its Christianity.

All along the East African coast the spiritual beliefs of Africa's indigenous people have become interwoven with the tenets of Arab immigrants. Old mosques and tombs may be relics of the Islamic tradition, but the power of their past is strong enough to attract people of any religious or animist persuasion. They, and the trees that surround them, create a vital link between the living and the dead. While Muslims once worshipped at the mosques, the trees overshadowing their ruins may now house the spirits of the ancestors of African animists, who still come to commune with these spirits. Nowhere are the edges between the animist spirituality of indigenous Africans and the Islamic beliefs of Arabs better blurred than in a grove of baobabs round an old Islamic town.

Some sacred sites, like the baobab on the Dar es Salaam waterfront, are taken over as trees of prayer and healing for the whole community. Others are the precincts of individual traditional doctors who may invoke help from spirits living in the tree or else summoned from further afield to give their assistance. Recognition of particular spirits may be confined to the minds of single communicants; otherwise several visitors may share similar experiences. I naively asked a healer in Mombasa how it happened that so many of her patients offered similar descriptions of a particular spirit, and, with a wave of her hand at the nearby tree, she replied simply, 'Because it's there'.

The Shrine of Saint Mary of Daarit in Eritrea may have saved the lives of Italian soldiers who sheltered there during a World War II bombardment of the town of Keren.

The statue of the Virgin Mary inside the consecrated baobab in Keren, Eritrea.

under the branches so that anyone arriving with evil intentions will either be recognized and disarmed by the tree spirits or will abandon any bad spirits to the tree on passing underneath it. During the construction of one of the causeways linking Mombasa Island to the mainland, workmen refused to cut down a baobab blocking the designated route. No-one, they contended, could order them to do something that would arouse such anger in the tree's occupying spirits; the causeway must be rerouted or they would stop work. Colonial administrators countered with the argument that the Government Spirit was far more powerful than the Baobab Spirit, and it

Was the act of pinning this scarf to a baobab trunk a plea for help, or a token of thanks for prayers answered? Could it have been pinned there during a healing ritual, or did someone simply bring their troubles and the scarf to the tree of their own accord?

An hour's drive north of Mombasa is Kilifi Creek, its south side edged by low cliffs of fossilized coral, above which are the grasslands and sisal fields of Kilifi Plantations. When supervising bush clearing one day, the farm's owner asked his foreman to be sure to preserve any young baobabs. The immediate response was that baobabs were seldom cut down anyway, as they were the resting place of *jinns*. The foreman then pointed to a young sapling, growing far out on its own, adding that no-one would ever cut that one down because its spirits had too far to jump to reach the next baobab, and so would possess its destroyer instead.

The foreman was a Giriama, who believe strongly that spirits, more often bad ones, occupy hollow baobabs. Village entrances are often sited

Baobabs growing around abandoned Islamic settlements may also be significant for the animist cultures along the East African coast (this is Gedi near Malindi in Kenya); the trees may even mark the sites of ancient graves.

would never lower itself to living in a tree. 'Seven days to quit' said a notice pinned to the baobab one morning, signed 'The Government Spirit'. On day eight the tree was felled.

However sacred trees may be, there is usually a way of bargaining with the spirits or appeasing the gods, so that the mighty giants of forest or savanna can be felled without fear of recrimination. Sometimes trees, or fish or mammals, must die so the tribe can survive, and the prayers before a tree is felled meld apology and appeasement with reverence and respect. This is no contradiction. When water began backing up behind the Kariba Dam, spirits inhabiting the doomed baobabs were successfully relocated, first by a ceremony of prayer and ritual, followed by tying branches from trees to be flooded onto others above the full water line.

Despite their otherworldliness, some gods and spirits are thought to require incentive or reward on Earth in exchange for their interventions, and the base of sacred trees may be heaped with offerings. Bottles, coconut husks, or the shells of large land snails laid at the bottom of a tree have usually held traditional alcohol, rose water or other liquids. Articles of clothing, once worn by the supplicant, may be left behind, perhaps in an attempt to shift sickness from the wearer to the tree, and then even onto another person. Occasionally money is offered up, presumably symbolically rather than in any real belief that good health or fertility actually has a price.

The first time I explored a sacred baobab near Kilifi, a pile of five- and ten-cent coins lay beside it. On my next visit to the tree, a few

A baobab growing out of the middle of the Baobab Café in Zanzibar.

months later, the money was gone. So, I said to myself, was the thief either so desperate he was prepared to risk incurable madness – the price of stealing from a shrine – for a few cents, or was he otherwise sure of the superior strength of his own juju? Then I became ashamed of such thoughts, and determined to accept that the healing spirit had simply collected its dues. That was better. Anyway, gifts of food or drink are meant to be shared with God or the resident spirits, and their disappearance from the foot of the tree is a sign that prayers have been heard.

In one of the streets of the old Stone Town in Zanzibar, rather appropriately called Mbuyuni Street, grows a fine old baobab,

now within the precincts of the Baobab Café. It forms the central pillar to the café and the trunk disappears out of sight in the middle of the red tin roof. There I met Fatma, a powerful Swahili woman who has lived in and around Stone Town for much of her life, and recalls this tree looming large over her childhood.

As a growing child, Fatma, together with her friends, would stop and play under the baobab in Mbuyuni Street, innocently searching for fallen fruit or flowers. When she reached puberty, her mother told Fatma that a bad spirit lived in the tree, which preyed upon young girls, never leaving once it had haunted them. Suitably alarmed, Fatma devised a new route home avoiding the tree. Many years later she began wondering why her mother had not mentioned the evil spirit earlier in her life. Why was she, Fatma, one of very few children who knew anything about it anyway? With neither parent alive to ask, she has now concluded that her mother wanted to stop her hanging around with boys by frightening her into finding a new way home. It would also not have escaped her mother that the tree was very close to the Persian Baths and on the days reserved for men, unsavoury characters would loiter around Mbuyuni Street.

Despite, or even because of, the natures of its spiritual occupants, there is great serenity beneath the spreading branches of a huge baobab tree. Is it only shade that brings that feeling of rest and relief, or is there something more? Have the elephants that once sheltered there from the midday sun or gouged away trunkfuls of moisture-laden fibre left behind some invisible reminders of their passing? Do vestiges of countless disputes settled by tribal elders still linger under the trees to help newcomers resolve their own differences? So many supplicants bringing the cares of their worlds to the base of a baobab must surely confer on that tree an aura of spiritual hope and expectation. A lot of baobabs have been around much longer than the great Christian cathedrals of northern Europe, and many of these trees have also served as places of worship. There is no escaping the incomparable sensation of stillness and tranquillity within an old church. It would be strange if similar feelings did not pervade the shade of ancient baobab trees.

There is an inescapable quietness and serenity beneath any ancient tree at the end of the day.

CHAPTER NINE

The baobab's destiny

The days when it was acceptable to set aside great swaths of land for the preservation of pristine natural environment, to the exclusion of all human beings, are largely over. Now it seems development is as inevitable in Africa as it is in any other part of the world. From the conservationist's perspective, one can hope that development is undertaken sensitively, minimizing both social and environmental upheaval. Yet the destruction of mature trees, and of their habitat, is one of the unavoidable consequences of almost any change in the use of previously untouched countryside.

Felling a giant

Of the many unplanned setbacks contributing to the failure of the Tanganyika Ground Nut Scheme, one of the first was the difficulty of converting thick African bush into peanut-growing plains. At Kongwa, baobabs posed the biggest problem. These ancient trees were pushed by giant earth movers, pulled by wheeled tractors, and even dynamited in an effort to complete the desolation and ensure nothing interrupted the military straightness of the crop lines. Only after a bulldozer dislodged a human skull from one of the trees did the Administration begin appreciating that the trees meant more to the local people than somewhere to hang a beehive or take refuge from the sun. In the end, however, what saved a pitiful scattering of the trees was not a sudden appreciation of their cultural, spiritual or aesthetic values, but rather the simple realization that they took up less space alive than felled.

The destruction of baobabs was also one of the prices paid for the conversion of lowland East African scrub into plantations of sisal. In West Africa and Sudan, baobabs came under threat because their wrinkled bark or fallen seed pods created refuges for insects that were harmful to cocoa or cotton crops. Mealy bugs spread viruses from baobabs to cocoa trees, while stainer bugs damaged cotton bolls in their search for oil in the seeds.

Localized felling of trees is inevitable when they are in the way of roads, airstrips, railways, electricity lines, mines, dams and other development. Seldom, though, is the desecration of baobabs so complete as to change the landscape forever. Planting sisal, cotton, cocoa and other crops has taken its toll, but the Ground Nut Scheme probably represents the greatest attempt ever to rub the baobab tree off a corner of its distribution map.

Initially, at least, small-scale cultivators usually spare baobabs, and the trees stand on as forlorn reminders of nature's original mosaic. As arable areas are passed from one generation to the next,

PREVIOUS PAGES: An idyllic African scene, but is this stunted baobab the only one for many kilometres around because other seedlings have never escaped the appetites of game animals confined in Tanzania's Lake Manyara National Park?

ABOVE: Many magnificent baobabs live on among the rows of sisal plants along the East African coast, but there is little sign in the plantations of the next generation of trees. Any seedlings will need careful nurturing if they are to survive.

This tree was being cut down to make way for a hut, but was spared at the last minute by the intervention of the local chief; several years on, it shows no ill effects from the gaping wound all round its trunk.

There are many economic arguments both for and against leaving baobabs standing on cultivated land, making it near impossible to arrive at irrefutable conclusions as to their net worth. The trees take up space that other plants could otherwise occupy. They reduce both solar light and rainfall by about half underneath the spread of their branches, and soil temperatures by several degrees. On the other hand, soil water content is higher in open land immediately after the start of rainy seasons, but it remains damper longer under the trees once rains have stopped. There are also more nutrients in the areas around the trees than out in the open.

The two-day demolition of a 1 000-year-old creation cannot seem other than a tragedy, both for its species as well as humanity. Even worse is the destruction of younger established trees, their huge potential to nourish the surrounding community as yet unfulfilled. Nonetheless, the real danger to the baobab's future comes much more from the destruction of seedlings or of habitat that would otherwise support them. Today, there is hardly an acre of African savanna, outside national parks and reserves, where too many domestic animals are not searching for too little grazing. Even within protected areas, game is often artificially confined by the closure of old dispersal routes with similar effect. So the seedlings and small trees that should eventually replace the great old landmarks find themselves victims of their own palatability.

and each son of a son inherits a smaller plot, the all-consuming baobabs are seen as taking up increasingly valuable space. If they must be cut down, they will be, without compunction. I would love to think of the tree as a pan-African symbol of resilience, a resting place for ancestral spirits, and a sacred source of strength and inspiration. Sadly, though, this would be romanticizing the truth. Throughout much of the continent the baobab is spared – not because it is hard to destroy, spiritually revered or a source of palatable fruit, but because the moist wood is unsuitable as building material, charcoal or firewood.

While the baobabs' preferred environment is on the dry side of average for African bush country, it may be well enough watered for its human inhabitants to imagine they can grow crops there. These people are often one-time pastoralists whose wanderings have gradually become restricted in the same way as those of the wild animals, their plight exacerbated by changes in government policies, and the sub-division of large tracts of communally held land into privately owned plots. Inevitably, the natural vegetation is replaced with sorghum, millet, okra, and sometimes maize. Even if these crops fail, the land will be grazed to the ground and baobabs are unlikely ever to grow again.

The next generation

In the course of my researches I counted and measured baobabs within two radically different areas of Kenya. The first survey was conducted on the lands of Kilifi Plantations, where many of the 1 200 baobabs we measured dominate permanent grass paddocks. Grazing by the dairy herd effectively ensures that the only seeds with any chance of growing into trees are those germinating in strips and gullies of uncultivated land beyond the pasture fences. The other survey was undertaken midway between Mombasa and Nairobi. Relatively recently settled, most of the big trees have been left in the fields, and small belts of natural riparian vegetation remain along the stream beds.

What emerged from both studies, with startling clarity, was a frightening dearth of very young trees. There were about as many very young as very old trees, when there should have been a massive natural surplus of young over older members of the species.

In addition to the destructive attentions of goats, gazelles or dairy herds, and the insidious shrinkage of their range as a result of human interference, baobabs are also starting to feel the heat of brush fires. Big baobabs, with their pachydermal skins, moisture-laden wood and amazing powers of recovery, can easily live on through fires inflaming the surrounding scrub. However, repeated burning of dead grass before each rainy season gives young seedlings little chance to attain the critical height and degree of resistance to survive the next fire.

ABOVE: Every picture tells a story; here, Hadzabe hunter-gatherers lament the destruction of a young baobab, felled by immigrant pastoralists (with no ancestral connection to this environment) so its leaves could be fed to their livestock.
OVERLEAF: Kilifi Plantations spared this huge tree as long as it could, but when the first branch fell onto a staff member's house one night (the occupant was away on leave), there was no option but to cut the other big branches.

Baobabs in full leaf look magnificent in the middle of the grasslands of Kilifi Plantations' dairy farm, but grazing cows prevent seedlings ever reaching tree size.

Lack of recruitment; where is the next generation? These themes recur both in scientific surveys, or in journeys through baobab country. Even allowing for the inevitable difficulty in finding young baobabs, the signs of young trees are disturbingly hard to discern.

The Kenyan Forestry Research Institute on the Nairobi-Mombasa road offers free indigenous trees to local farmers. Among the assorted species are baobabs, neatly packaged in pots made from half a pod of their own fruit. Given the choice, farmers usually reject the offer of a free baobab, almost as though fearing invasion by unwelcome spirits, but in truth because they perceive the trees as useless. If they really believe baobabs have been around since 'Noah's time', as a Wakamba

LEFT AND RIGHT: These photographs show the same tree: the one on the right taken a year or so after the one on the left. In the interim, the baobab's top has been grazed off by elephants in search of dry-season food – something that must, ultimately, affect the shape of the mature tree.

ABOVE: This tree is growing out of a low cliff and is older than its size suggests. Many years ago, when more baobabs grew around this end of Lake Manyara, baboons probably deposited the seed from which it emerged. **OVERLEAF:** These *Adansonia grandidieri* look magnificent pushing their way up above the Malagasy horizon, but they are, in fact, sorry relics of a flattened forest.

woman once told me, perhaps they also consider any benefit a young tree might eventually offer is simply too remote to contemplate.

Some 500 years ago, the Dogon people arrived at the bottom of the cliffs forming the Bandiagara escarpment in Mali, driving out the Tellem tribe, which then inhabited the area. The Dogon were probably responding to the spread of Islam around the edges of their ancestral territories, as well as to the slave raids from which the cliffs of their new home offered protection. The flood plains below the cliffs also provided fertile ground for crops, and it is said the Dogon were led there by a huge serpent that also showed them streams, waterfalls, and the many uses of the baobab tree.

So man depended on tree, and this in itself insured its future, at least until the early 20th century, when the spread of European influence began to unbalance the continent. The Dogon are still there today, as are the *Oro* (baobabs), which have provided a stable source of wild food ever since the invaders' arrival. However, populations of both Dogon and their livestock are now expanding dramatically, and competition for dwindling natural resources is unrelenting. The desert is encroaching fast: now there is almost nothing but sand dunes beyond the flood plains.

The modern ease of communication and travel are slowly severing the bonds that bind man to his immediate environment. With Africa's ever-expanding population, areas of land need to support increasing numbers of human inhabitants and their animal dependants. Once an area is full, people move onto other land with which they have no ancestral connection at all. This was evident as we researched the baobabs in Kibwezi,

near the Research Institute. The area was settled in the 1960s by Wakamba from far away, where no baobabs grew. Arriving with no spiritual, ethnobotanical or nutritional experience of the trees, the only value they could place on them was nuisance. If the trees were too much work to cut down, they were certainly not worth replacing when they eventually toppled over. The same scenario applies to the Hadzabe, whose traditional homelands are being squeezed on all sides by onion farmers, conservationists and incoming pastoralists with little understanding of, and no connection to, their new environment.

The sense of permanence that once joined successive generations to the same area of land is slowly disintegrating. As a result, the responsibility to hold that land as trustee for the next generation is vanishing. In its place is the notion of absolute ownership, which itself implies a right to exploit for the present with no thought for the future. The traditional ties that bound a community together are continually being loosened, and unless there is a personal and present benefit from planting trees, there is little incentive to do so.

At the same time, the animist credo linking man with his environment through the belief that trees and animals harboured their own spirits is disappearing. As a result, the protection afforded these natural spiritual resting places has also disappeared. Abandoned animist beliefs may perhaps be replaced by an adherence to conventional religions, but in most of these nature plays an insignificant role.

Natural regeneration depends not only on man's wise management of the land where the trees might grow, but also on the continued attentions of pollinators and seed-dispersers. Bats still seem to be doing their work, as they are able to adapt to life in and around human habitations. Seed-dispersers are faring less well.

Perhaps some African farmers think that any benefits baobabs may eventually bestow are just too many years away to make them worthwhile planting. There were no takers for baobabs at this indigenous tree nursery in Kenya, even though they were being given away.

While the all important baboons manage to survive on rocky hillsides, their presence is scarcely compatible with subsistence farming, and crop-raiding monkeys find it increasingly difficult to forage successfully.

Lake Manyara is a soda lake at the foot of the escarpment up which slants the road to the Serengeti. Down towards the south end of the lake is a hot spring, Maji Moto ('hot water' in Swahili). Above the spring is a jumble of rocks, and a single, gnarled little baobab leans out over the lake edge, its roots scarcely distinguishable from the stone surfaces they snake over. I watched a party of buffalo graze contentedly on the lush grass all around the spring, backed by pink clusters of flamingos filtering out algae along the lake edge. It was an idyllic African landscape, although one with no other visible baobabs for many kilometres in any direction. Perhaps a millennium ago baboons dropped seeds there, one of which became that twisted, rock-clinging baobab. But where are all the other descendants of the trees from which those baboons feasted during their lives?

Breeding trees

Given the benefits provided by mature baobabs, it is not surprising that individuals and institutions are trying to coax shoots out of the dark brown baobab seeds. In 1764, the 7th edition of *Miller's Gardener's Dictionary* gave advice on propagating baobabs in England, where they were, 'too tender to thrive in this Country without this artificial Heat, therefore they must constantly remain in the Stove with other exotic Plants'. Getting seedlings going in modern Africa is a lot less arduous, and nursery-bred baobabs are joining the next generation. In Mali, baobab domestication programmes are under way. In an attempt to meld modern science with local knowledge, and in so doing breed the best trees, scientists analyze the vitamin C content of baobab fruit of different sizes and shapes, then try to correlate the results with the traditional division of trees according to bark colour or fruit taste.

Breeding trees is not the work for anyone in a hurry, and selectively breeding baobabs even less so. As baobabs take 20 or 30 years to mature, tracing distinctive characteristics from one generation to the next is a frustratingly slow process. Throughout Africa, persuading local people to invest time and energy in caring for slow-growing baobabs often entails an extensive reappraisal of their community's natural heritage.

Buoyed by the accumulated experience of the International Centre for Research in Agroforestry, whose computerized database informed that after suitable pre-treatment seeds may take only six days to germinate, and that germination is usually 90–100%, I tried to breed some trees. I began by planting five batches of 100 seeds, each in separate boxes. One batch was planted straight from a newly fallen pod, and another from the perfect environment of a cracked pod, into which invading insects had introduced damp soil. The third batch was covered with boiling water and soaked for 24 hours before planting, and all those in the fourth were first lightly cracked with pliers. The remaining 100 seeds I had painstakingly picked from baboon faeces beside the Athi River. After ten months, two shoots had appeared from these 500 seeds. Both died, and it was little consolation to read that experiments at the Royal Botanic Gardens in Kew had been even less successful.

Baobabs are usually bred from seeds but will grow from carefully nurtured cuttings too. They can also be transplanted much later in life, and anyone wishing to reinforce their belief in baobabs being born big, overnight, should have been in Kasane in northern Botswana one day in 1995. The Mowana Hotel was struck by lightning in 1993, and with it burnt the eponymous baobab. If the rebuilt hotel was to keep its name, it had to have a baobab. How? Simply dig up a big tree, lift it with a crane onto a low loader and install it in the middle of the courtyard. It now looks as if it had lived there all its life, and is so large that the outstretched arms of five men could barely encircle its trunk.

Enduring trees

Baobabs cast their shadows over a continent in transition, where huts give way to houses, horses to horsepower, dirt trails to tarred highways. While the trees stand witness to many hundreds of years of human behaviour, they leave no trace of their own passing, being poor subjects for fossilization, and drying to dust soon after their roots finally cease to channel up water. The living trees speak for the species, not their remains.

Today, the speed of environmental change is such that those plants and animals slow to adapt may be left behind on some ecological scrap heap – doomed relics of a former age. It is far too soon to commission the Requiem for the Baobab Tree, or to start ensuring that the species is represented in every tropical city's botanical garden. It is impossible to think of baobabs as remotely endangered, as they are spread so prominently over such a wide area. Nonetheless, droughts, overgrazing and land clearing are taking a relentless toll. If baobabs cannot adapt, the descendants of today's trees may be left to try and find rootholds in rocky clefts, coral rag,

and other places where hungry herbivores fear to tread. In 200 years most of the African landscape presently dominated by baobabs will look very different. Will wild baobabs in natural settings, like most of the continent's large mammals, then only be experienced in enclosed little pockets of protected countryside?

It is too easy, and almost *de rigueur*, to end any conservation story on a note of alarm, and enough warning bells have already been rung.

Perhaps the best-known group of baobabs in Africa is that known as Baines' Baobabs, growing on a tiny islet in Botswana's Kidiakam Pan, a salty lake-bed dry for ten months a year. Thomas Baines painted the trees in May 1862. The baobabs have been visited many times since, by those keen to compare the living trees with their painted depiction, and by me in November 2004. Typically for baobabs on the edges of Botswana's dried pans, these ones showed themselves from far away as much the tallest things in their landscape. The sun had almost set and the trees had to compete for our attentions with a dozen elephants splashing around in a muddy pool

of three-day-old rainwater. Reaching the trees entailed skirting round the edge of a dried saltpan across which hundreds of wildebeest and zebra were making their seemingly aimless way. Their hooves crunched on the cracked surface, belying the soft mud below.

All the baobabs are still there, just as they were painted and, much more importantly, so are lots of young ones. Even the fallen giant that had so intrigued Baines was putting out leafy shoots. A barn owl flew silently around the trees, and it was still light enough for this to set smaller birds, settling down to roost, into an agitated twitter. Squeaks came from the owl's hole, young ones perhaps, and maybe even descended from forebears that swooped around the fire while Thomas Baines laid his bearded head on whatever passed for a pillow. When the last of these huge historic trees has sucked up its final drop of water, to be remembered only in paintings, photographs and commemorative postage stamps, the young trees will have grown up to take the place of their famous ancestors, and a clump of baobabs will still break the distant horizon.

PREVIOUS PAGES: Baines' Baobabs, in Botswana, are seldom photographed with water around their island, not least because of the difficulty in reaching them in the rainy season.
ABOVE: There are enough young baobabs growing among the older ones to ensure that in 500 years' time a clump of these wonderful trees will still be seen from far across the Kidiakam Pan.
BELOW: Thomas Baines' sketch of the baobabs that still bear his name 150 years later.
(With permission, Royal Geographical Society, London)

Acknowledgements

Baobabs have loomed especially large over my life ever since I hiked along the bottom of the Dogon Escarpment in Mali, seven years ago. Despite having lived in East Africa for nearly 30 years, with the nearest baobab two-and-a-half hours' drive away (it used to be 15 minutes less but the Nairobi–Mombasa road has recently been realigned), only in Mali did I begin to appreciate how vital these trees can sometimes be to the people living around them.

I started this book soon after my return to Kenya from West Africa. Since then I have had wonderful experiences around baobab trees in many parts of this extraordinary continent. These experiences, my researches and the time spent writing, have inspired a much better understanding of both tree ecology and the relationship between trees and people.

Now, I can look back down the long road of this book's writing with a view of rain clouds building up over the Ngong Hills, and the staccato chorus of chestnut weavers in the thorn trees above the pond. And, at last, I can stop asking for favours, and start thanking the many people along the way who have helped me in my travels and research.

If Malcolm Linton and Linda de Souza had not lived in Abidjan, so providing a reason to visit West Africa and a base from which to reach Mali, it is highly unlikely this book would ever have been written. Thank you both for being the catalyst for its creation. In Namibia, travelling companions Eddy de Buysscher and Phil Karber indulged my urge to visit outposts of baobab territory with the best of grace. On a later visit to Namibia, a childhood friend and true English eccentric, David Leishman, entertained us in the Caprivi Strip to a lot more than just a visit to the baobab loo in Katima Mulilo. In Botswana, Alec Campbell gave hospitality and access to his huge store of knowledge of baobabs and all else in his home country. Hugh Glen helped me from Zimbabwe and it was some time before I was able to return the favours in Kenya.

In Tanzania, visiting Sally Perry and Franco Paglieri on their farm near Mtwara, on the Mozambique border, was one of the earliest of many memorable experiences in that country. David and Deborah Haworth provided a wonderful base at Kilombero from which to explore Baobab Valley. Friedrich Alpers always took an interest in the book's progress from his outpost in the Selous, while Tony and Lucy Fitzjohn welcomed us to Mkomazi, as did Bim Theobald to Dar es Salaam (no blame on him for my being mugged on the beach there). Tor Allan and Sarah Henderson sustained me in Arusha before I set off for Lake Eyasi to see the Hadzabe people that live around it.

From Madagascar, Gary Lemmer sent me snippets of baobabilia, and his hotel in Morondava was an ideal base from which to visit the Kirindy Forest and the Avenue du Baobab en route. Further north, Francesca Calini found us baobabs on islands so remote it seemed ours were the first footprints ever to dent their sands. From Australia, Nicola Smyth sent me information about the eighth member of the genus and Tony Cunningham gave of his knowledge and experiences of Africa.

Christopher Wilson threw open his Kilifi farm for research and his house for rest as well as recruiting Joyce Bundotich and Irene Maundu to measure and count trees, and other helpers to dig up root systems and guide me round that beautiful piece of Kenya. Joshua Muli helped my research in the field in Kibwezi, as did Richard Ambani in the National Archives in Nairobi.

In Kenya, many other friends gave help in different forms – information, pictures and hospitality, which all contributed in one way or another to my finalizing this book. In particular I would like to thank Sue Allan, Renzo Bernardi, Peter and Grete Davey, Charles Dewhurst, Robert Foster, Jeannie Knocker, Oscar Mann, Dino Martins, Max Morgan-Davies, Mary O'Reilly, and Anne Powys, with a special thanks to Len Newton for allowing me to tap the rich vein of his botanical knowledge. The staff of Kenya Forestry Research Institute at Gedi provided me with access to the baobab plantation there; Bettina Schoop of GTZ arranged a visit to basket weavers in Mwingi; Chuck Benough found an increment borer; Janet Manuel explained how to extract oil from baobab seeds, and George and Philippa Corse cooked an exquisite dinner of fresh baobab produce.

Some of my correspondents I have yet to meet, including Gary Clarke, Ed Eastwood, Edward Fletcher, Doreen Hartley, Mike Kimberley, Mike McGraw, Siyakah Mguni, Hannah Nadel, Lola Stephen, Jutta von Breitenbach of the Dendrological Society in South Africa, Heather van Heerden and Ian Whyte. Others, like Edward Paice, I have only met once. Thank you all, and I hope that, one way or another, you at least get to hear that the work to which you contributed has finally found its place on the bookshop shelf.

If David Coulson, Rowena White and other helpers at Kenya Trust for African Rock Art had not scanned a selection of my slides so expertly this book might have remained unpublished much longer. Nigel Pavitt showed his technical wizardry in scanning photographs, and Bridget McGraw showed hers in researching and downloading illustrations and generally being a computer whizz.

Many friends offered illustrations, some of which have appeared in this book, and, whether they have or not, thanks to all of you for sharing these and for often going to considerable trouble to get them to me.

It has been my happy experience that the staff of libraries and other centres of research are always prepared to go that little bit further in their efforts to help. Those of Nairobi's Herbarium, British Institute in Eastern Africa, the International Centre for Research in Agroforestry, Royal Botanic Gardens in Kew, Royal Geographical Society in London, Botswana National Museum, Kirstenbosch National Botanical Garden, University of Namibia and the National Botanical Research Institute's Tree Atlas project in Windhoek all made me feel there was nowhere else I would rather be than in one of their library chairs. In my search for pictures, the illustrations departments of some of the above were equally helpful, as was that in the Hunt Institute for Botanical Documentation.

I reserve my expressions of greatest gratitude to two eminent experts on *Adansonia*, who shared their knowledge with unhesitating generosity. Gerald Wickens, formerly of Kew and author of that institution's fine publication, *The Baobab – Africa's Upside-Down Tree,* answered endless, often rather naive, questions both in person at his Norfolk home and through email, all while writing his own *magnum opus* on the tree. In America, David Baum has published many papers on *Adansonia* and probably knows more about the genus as a whole than anyone else on Earth, and he, too, gave of his enormous store of scientific knowledge – and of his brilliant illustrations – with equal magnanimity.

Tom Heaton, Imre Loefler and John Millard, I bored you all about baobabs for long enough, and it is a real sadness that none of you is around to see the fruits of all those conversations; nevertheless, you are all here in the pages as, John, is one of your photographs.

Much of this travel was undertaken in the company of my other half, Mary Ann, who senses things in trees I never do, and now uses their healing properties in her work. We have marvelled at hundreds of baobab trees together, as I know we will continue to do, notwithstanding the birth of this book.

This is the expurgated version, the manuscript having once reached a length of 80 000 words before being almost chopped in half. This was a difficult exercise, but only I know what isn't in it any more, as was pointed out to cheer me up after Pippa Parker of the publishers asked me to wield the big scissors. No less thanks are due to those who provided gems that no longer shine in the final text, and I hope a chance will arise to use them at a later date.

I end with a botanical footnote. I am well aware that Africa has lost the battle with Australia for the right to use the genus name of *Acacia*; however, I continue to use the old names for members of this genus, not through any sense of scientific stubbornness, but simply because these will continue in use in Africa for many years to come.

Baobabs in Tsavo, Kenya, are in full leaf during the rainy season in November and December. The tree hanging over the Tsavo River is a doum palm (*Hyphaene compressa*).

Selected bibliography

References to baobabs are many and varied. A lot of them, especially the more recent, are easily available at the press of a search inquiry button. Those below, grouped under appropriate subject matter headings, are most of the ones that have helped me in writing this book, and are generally not on view on the Internet. Their inclusion serves not only to guide future researchers but also to acknowledge, with grateful thanks, other people's efforts.

Quite the best general introduction to the tree is:

Wickens, GE. (1982) *The Baobab – Africa's Upside Down Tree – Kew Bulletin,* Vol. 37, 2, which also has an excellent bibliography.

Some general works on trees:

Beentje, HJ. (1988) Fig Trees (*Ficus* Moracaceae) of Kenya – *Journal of the East Africa Natural History Society and National Museum,* Vol. 76.

Coates Palgrave, K. (1981) *Trees of Southern Africa* – Struik Publishers, Cape Town.

Exell, AW & Wild, H. (1961) *Flora Zambesica* – Crown Agents, London.

Jacobson, H. (1960) *Handbook of Succulent Plants* – Kiel Botanical Gardens.

Noad, TC & Birnie, A. (1989) *Trees of Kenya* – Published privately, Nairobi.

Pakenham, T. (1996) *Meetings with Remarkable Trees* – George Weidenfeld & Nicholson, London.

Pakenham, T. (2002) *Remarkable Trees of the World* – Weidenfeld & Nicholson, London.

Palmer, E & Pitman, N. (1972) *Trees of Southern Africa* – AA Balkema, Cape Town.

Roodt, V. (1998) *Trees & Shrubs of the Okavango Delta* – Shell Oil, Botswana.

Setshogo, MP & Venter, F. (2003) Trees of Botswana; Names and Distribution – *Southern African Botanical Diversity Network Report,* Vol. 18, Pretoria.

Thomas, P. (2000) *Trees; Their Natural History* – Cambridge University Press.

Van Wyk, P. (1984) *Field Guide to the Trees of the Kruger National Park* – Struik Publishers, Cape Town.

Early historical references before the age of British exploration and referred to in this book include:

Alpini, P. (1592) *De plantis Aegypti liber* – Venice.

Adanson, M. (1757) *Histoire naturelle du Senegal* – Paris.

Battuta, I. (1325–1354) *Travels of Ibn Battuta* – Hakluyt Society, 4 volumes.

Cadamosto. (1455) *Voyages of Cadamosto* – Hakluyt Society Series 2, Vol. 80.

Darwin, C. (1859) *The Origin of Species* – Reprinted, London.

Miller, P. (1764) *Miller's Gardener's Dictionary* – London.

Ray, J. (1691) *The Wisdom of God Manifested in the Works of Creation* – London.

Once British explorers set foot on the Dark Continent, few passed baobabs without describing them in the memoirs of their expeditions; among the plethora of these, those below pay particular attention to the trees:

Baines, T. (1864) *Explorations in S W Africa* – Longman, London.

Baines, T. (1946) *The Northern Goldfields: Diaries of Thomas Baines* – Chatto & Windus, London.

Barth, H. (1857) *Travels and Discoveries in North and Central Africa in the years 1849–1855* – Longman, London.

Burton, R. (1860) *The Lake Regions of Central Africa* – Longman, London.

Cameron, VL. (1885) *Across Africa* – George Philip & Son, London.

Chapman, J. (1868) *Travels in the Interior of South Africa* – Bell & Daldy, London.

Johnston, HH. (1897) *British Central Africa* – Methuen & Co, London.

Junker, W. (1890) *Travels in Africa* – Chapman & Hall, London.

Keynes, Q. (1959) Dr Livingstone's Monogram I Presume? – *Personality* Magazine, Oct 8.

Livingstone, D. (1857) *Missionary Travels and Researches in South Africa* – John Murray, London.

Livingstone, D & Livingstone, C. (1865) *Narrative of an Expedition to the Zambesi and its Tributaries* – John Murray, London.

Maugham, RCF. (1910) *Zambezia* – John Murray, London.

Sikes, SK. (1972) *Lake Chad* – Eyre Methuen, London.

Among publications on the evolution of *Adansonia* and its distribution outside Africa are:

Armstrong, P. (1977) Baobabs; remnant of Gondwanaland? – *New Scientist,* Vol. 73.

Armstrong, P. (1983) The disjunct distribution of the genus *Adansonia* – *The National Geographical Journal of India,* Vol. 29.

Baden-Powell, BH. (1878/9) The Baobab Tree in South Punjab – *Indian Forester,* Vol. 4.

Baum, DA. (1994) A Review of Chromosome Numbers in *Bombacaceae* with New Counts for *Adansonia* – *Taxon,* 43,1.

Baum, DA. (1996) The Ecology and Conservation of the Baobabs of Madagascar – *Primate Report,* 46,1.

Baum, DA et al. (1998) Biogeography and Floral Evolution of Baobabs as Inferred from Multiple Data Sets – *Systematic Biology,* Vol. 47(2).

Bowman, DMJS. (1997) Observations on the demography of the Australian boab in the north-west of the Northern Territory, Australia – *Australian Journal of Botany,* Vol. 45,5.

Burton-Page, J. (1969) The problem of the introduction of *Adansonia digitata* into India – in domestication and exploitation of plants and animals, Gerald Duckworth, London.

Du Puy, B. (1996) The Baobabs of Madagascar – *Curtis's Botanical Magazine,* Vol. 13,2.

Glen, HF & Hardy, DS. (1992) Baobabs: Fathers of the Forest – *Trees in South Africa,* Oct–March.

Humbert, H. (1955) Flore de Madagascar – Typographie Firmin-Didot, Paris.

Jackson, JR. (1868) The Gouty Stem Tree – *The Student and Intellectual Observer,* Vol. 1.6.

Jumelle, H & Perrier, H. (1914) Les Baobabs de Madagascar – *Bibliothèque d'agriculture coloniale,* Paris.

Leriche, A. (1954) Autour du mot baobab – *Notes Africaines,* Vol. 63.

Lowe, P. (1998) *The Boab Tree* – Lothian Books, Melbourne.

Maheshwari, JK. (1971) The Baobab Tree; Disjunctive Distribution and Conservation – *Biological Conservation,* Vol. 4,1.

Newton, LE. (1980) Phytogeographical Associations of the Succulent Plant Flora of South-west Arabia and the Horn of Africa – *National Cactus & Succulent Journal,* Vol. 35,4.

Roxburgh, W. (1832) *Flora Indica* – Serampore, Calcutta.

Vaid, KM. (1978) Where is the mythical 'wishing tree'? – *Science Today,* April.

Varmah, JC & Vaid, KM. (1964) Baobab – The Historic African Tree at Allahabad – *The Indian Forester,* Vol. 104,7.

Webber, T. (1902) *The Forests of Upper India* – Edward Arnold.

Many books and papers focus on baobabs and mankind, whether in historical contexts, or from a more ethnobotanical angle, some of which are:

Abbiw, DK. (1990) *The Useful Plants of Ghana* – Intermediate Technology Publications & Royal Botanic Gardens, Kew, London.

Adam, JG. (1962) Le Baobab (*Adansonia digitata*) – *Notes Africaines,* Vol. 94.

Balick, MJ & Cox, PA. (1996) *Plants, People and Culture – The science of ethnobotany* – Scientific American Library, New York.

Blunt, HS. (1923) Tebeldis – *Sudan Notes and Records,* Vol. 6.

Craig, S. (1997) – Hell and High Water – *The Geographical Magazine,* 1996.

Dalziel, JM. (1937) *The Useful Plants of West Tropical Africa* – Crown Agents, London.

French, MH. (1944) Composition and Nutritive Value of Pulp and Seeds in the Fruit of the Baobab – *East African Agricultural Journal.*

Hobley, CW. (1922) On Baobabs and Ruins – *Journal of the East Africa and Uganda Natural History Society.*

Lloyd, W. (1910) Tebeldis – *Geographical Journal.*

Mauny, R. (1951) L'origine du mot baobab – *Notes Africaines,* Vol. 50.

Migeod, FWH. (1924) *Through Nigeria to Lake Chad* – Heath Cranton, London.

Migeod, FWH. (1912) *Through Timbuktu and across the Great Sahara* – Seley Service & Co, London

Mshigeni, KE & Hangula L. (2001) *Africa's Baobab Resources – Unlocking their economic potential* – University of Namibia.

Newbold, D. (1924) More Notes on Tebeldis – *Sudan Notes and Records,* Vol. 7.

Nour, AA et al. (1980) Chemical composition of baobab fruit – *African Science,* Vol. 22,4.

Owen, J. (1970) The medico-social and cultural significance of *Adansonia digitata* in African Communities – *African Notes,* Vol. 6,1.

Owen, R. (1971) *Saga of the Niger* – Robert Hale, London.

Pakenham, T. (2004) *The Remarkable Baobab* – Weidenfeld, London.

Rashford, J. (1986) The Baobab Tree and Seasonal Hunger in Africa – the Case of the San – *Botswana Notes and Records,* Vol. 19.

Schultes, RE & von Reis, S. (1995) *Ethnobotany, Evolution of a Discipline* – Chapman & Hall, London.

Sibide, M et al. (1996) Baobab – Homegrown Vitamin C for Africa – *Agroforestry Today,* April.

Sweeney, C. (1973) *Background of Baobabs* – Constable, London.

Szolnoki, TW. (1985) *Food and Fruit Trees of the Gambia* – Intermediate Technology Publications & Royal Botanic Gardens, Kew, London.

Tothill, JD, Editor. (1954) *Agriculture in the Sudan* – Oxford University Press, London.

Van Beek, WEA & Banga, PM. (1992) The Dogon and their Trees – Chapter 4 in *Bush Base; Forest Farm, Culture, Environment & Development* – Routledge, London.

Watt, JM & Breyer-Brandwijk, MG. (1962) *Medicinal and Poisonous Plants of Southern and Eastern Africa* – E S Livingstone, London.

Wickens, GE. (1979) The Uses of the Baobab in Africa – Proceedings 9 of Plenary Meeting of AETFAT, Las Palmas.

Wood, A. (1950) *The Groundnut Affair* – Bodley Head, London.

The last word on taxonomy is contained in:

Baum, DA. (1995) A systematic revision of *Adansonia* (Bombacaceae) – *Annals of the Missouri Botanical Garden,* Vol. 82.

Some papers on age, size and growth:

Adam, JG. (1963) Le Plus Gros Baobab du Senegal n'est plus celui de Dakar – *Notes Africaines,* Vol. 98.

Carr, JD. (1970) How Old is that Baobab? – *Trees in South Africa,* Vol. 22,3.

Friede, HM. (1964) Radiocarbon Estimation of the Age of Indigenous Trees – *Trees in South Africa*, Vol. 16,2.

Guy, GL. (1970) *Adansonia digitata* and its rate of growth in relation to rainfall in South Central Africa – *Proceedings and transactions of Rhodesia Scientific Association*, Vol. 54,2.

Guy, GL. (1974) Notes on Baobabs – *South African Forestry Journal*, Vol. 89.

Lewington, A & Parker, E. (1999) *Ancient Trees – Trees that live for a thousand years* – Collins & Brown, London.

Mullin, LJ. (1991) The baobab – giant of Zimbabwe's lowveld – *Excelsa*, Vol. 15.

Struve, KCP. (1925) The Age of Tebeldis – *Sudan Notes and Records*, Vol. 8.

Swart, ER. (1963) Age of the Baobab Tree – *Nature*, Vol. 198.

Von Breitenbach, F. (1982) National Register of Big Trees – *Journal of Dendrology*, Vol. 2.

Von Breitenbach, F. (1985) National Register of Big Trees; the first three years – *Journal of Dendrology,* Vol. 5.

Wilson, RT. (1988) Vital statistics of the baobab – *African Journal of Ecology*, Vol. 26.

Elephants and baobabs have received their share of attention, particularly in:

Barnes, RFW. (1980) The decline of the baobab tree in Ruaha National Park, Tanzania – *African Journal of Ecology,* Vol. 18.

Caughley, G. (1976) The elephant problem – an alternative hypothesis – *East African Wildlife Journal,* Vol. 14.

Guy, PR. (1982) Baobabs and elephants – *African Journal of Ecology*, Vol. 20.

Napier Bax, P & Sheldrick, DLW. (1963) Some preliminary observations on the food of elephant in the Tsavo Royal National Park (East) of Kenya – *East African Wildlife Journal,* Vol. 1.

Swanepoel, CM. (1993) Baobab damage in Mana Pools National Park, Zimbabwe – *African Journal of Ecology*, Vol. 31.

Swanepoel, CM & SM. (1986) – Baobab damage by elephant in the middle Zambesi Valley, Zimbabwe – *African Journal of Ecology*, Vol. 24.

Watson, RWM. (2001) The Mingled Destinies of Baobabs and Elephants – *Swara, Journal of East African Wild Life Society*, Vol. 24,1.

Weyerhaeuser, FJ. (1985) Survey of elephant damage to baobabs in Tanzania's Lake Manyara National Park – *African Journal of Ecology,* Vol. 23.

Whyte, I. (c. 2000) *Baobabs and Elephants in the Kruger National Park* – private publication.

Other publications on general biology and ecology:

De Villiers, PC. (1951) Die Kremetartboom – *Journal of South African Forestry Association*, Vol. 20.

Newton, L. (1974) Is the Baobab Tree Succulent? – *Cactus and Succulent Journal of Great Britain*, Vol. 36,3.

Owen, J. (1970) A contribution to the ecology of the African Baobab – *Savanna*, Vol. 3,1.

Simpson, M. (1995) The Ecology of the Baobab – a literature review – Thesis for School of Agricultural and Forest Sciences, University of Wales, Bangor.

Verdoorn, IC. (1969) The Baobab or Kremetartboom – *African Wild Life*.

Von Breitenbach, F. (1974) Baobab Flower – *Trees in South Africa*, Vol. 24.

And pollination:

Baum, DA. (1995) The Comparative Pollination and Floral Biology of Baobabs – *Annals of the Missouri Botanical Garden*, Vol. 82.

Coe, MJ & Isaac, FM. (1965) Pollination of the Baobab by the Lesser Bush Baby – *East African Wildlife Journal*, Vol. 3.

Harris, BJ & Baker, HG. (1959) Pollination of flowers by bats in Ghana – *Nigerian Field*, 24.

Kock, D. (1972) Fruit-bats and Bat-flowers – *East African Natural History Society Bulletin*, July.

Meuse, B & Morris, S. (1984) *The Sex Life of Flowers* – Faber & Faber, London.

Proctor, M et al. (1996) *The Natural History of Pollination* – Harper Collins, London (New Naturalist Series).

Start, AN. (1972) Pollination of the baobab by the fruit bat *Rousettus aegypticus* – *East African Wildlife Journal*, Vol. 10.

Finally, something for the spirit:

Abungu, GH. (1994) Islam on the Kenyan coast: an overview of Kenyan coastal sacred sites – in *Sacred Sites, Sacred Places,* Routledge, London.

Boyer, M-F. (1996) *Tree Talk – Memories, Myths and Timeless Customs* – Thames & Hudson, London.

Friede, HM. (1953) Trees in Rock Paintings – *Trees in South Africa*, Vol. 5,3.

Giles, L. (1982) Mbaraki Pillar and its Spirits – *Kenya Past and Present,* Vol. 19.

Godfrey, D. (1969) *The Peoples of Zanzibar; Their Customs and Religious Beliefs* – Negro Universities Press, New York.

Harvey, PH. (1970) Trees and Rock Art – *Trees in South Africa*, Vol. 22,1.

Mauny, R. (1955) Baobabs – cimetières à griots – *Notes Africaines*, Vol. 67.

Mbiti, JS. (1969) *African Religions and Philosophy* – Heineman.

Mutoro, HW. (1994) The Mijikenda kaya as a sacred site – in *Sacred Sites, Sacred Places,* Routledge, London.

Many of the baobabs on Lekhubu Island in Botswana defy conventional thoughts on how trees should be shaped.

Index
Page references in italics
indicate illustrations.

The consecrated baobab in Eritrea.

The remains of a settlement at Jumba la Mtwana.

The author hiking through baobabs along the Dogon escarpment in Mali.